You're It!

You're It!

Shared Wisdom for Successfully
Leading Organizations
From Both a Seasoned and a First-Time CEO

Alan Broadbent & Franca Gucciardi

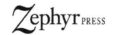

CONTENTS

INTRODUCTION

FRANCA: In 2004, I received a phone call from the Loran Scholars Foundation asking me to consider the role of CEO. When it came, I thought that everything I had done to that point had prepared me to say yes. But then came the questions. Was I ready to take on this first major CEO role? Was I too young? I was only thirty-three, at least fifteen years younger than the person in the position. Was the Loran Scholars Foundation the right organization for my first CEO role?

At the time of the call, I was director of the Millennium Excellence Awards, a federally funded program I had helped to design and implement. I knew how to manage people, both volunteers and paid staff, oversee large budgets, and develop business plans, processes, and workflows. In short, I had experience in managing large undertakings successfully, but I wondered if this was enough to take on the leadership of an organization. After all, I had never had financial responsibility for an organization. I called a few of my mentors. That was when I called Alan and asked, "How do you know when you are ready?"

I did take on the position. Just weeks into the job, I realized the immense task ahead of me, and I went to see Alan. Unlike others around the organization who had no qualms about telling me exactly what I should do, my conversations with Alan were different. He was never directive. He simply listened and had a knack for asking me just the question I needed to contemplate at the time. He became my trusted advisor, and I began meeting with him every few months as I thought through the different stages of my work.

ALAN: I remember those first meetings. I knew Franca from my involvement as a member of the Loran board, and as its first non-executive chair, a position I took over from Loran founder, Bob Cluett. I'd been close to the organization through its governance, and also because its Toronto office was, for several years, across the hall from our Maytree and Avana Capital offices.

The meetings with Franca were very interesting for me because I could see her growing into her leadership. As a former Loran scholar, she had the basic attributes we looked for in our selection process: leadership, character, and community engagement. Typical of Loran scholars, these skills were raw materials with the potential to be refined into higher-level skills.

From the leadership work we've done at Maytree, I knew that leaders could be made. There may be some "born leaders," but most good leaders have picked up the skills through experience and over time. At Maytree we've always liked the idea of collapsing time frames, so that what might naturally happen in ten years can happen in three, or even two. This can be achieved through teaching and mentorship, and by focusing on the necessary skill sets.

Good leaders need some basics: an ability to think through issues to solutions and not be paralyzed by complexity; flexibility and a high tolerance for ambiguity; and what I've always called bravery, a willingness to take responsibility and be accountable.

Ultimately, a good leader has to come up with the right answers. Answers are important. But the road to good answers runs through the right questions. Over the years, as I've worked with developing leaders, knowing what questions to ask is often most useful. These are questions that lead to good answers and prevent wallowing in inquiry.

This is how my conversations with Franca developed. I knew she had the basics. What we did was figure out what the questions were. I'd listen to her describe the issues and problems she was facing, and together we'd reframe them as questions she needed to answer.

Was it tempting to answer those questions for her? It certainly was. But I think that an answer to a question, or a solution to a problem, is more durable when we have to do the work ourselves, thinking our way through it and designing how we might implement the solution. The process gives us more ownership of the solution and a deeper understanding.

FRANCA AND ALAN: After a few years, we recognized that our conversations would be useful to anyone facing a first-time role as CEO. We know there are numerous books on leadership and management, but these can be a bit over-whelming for someone new to leading an organization. Simply put, you need time or experience to be able to read through some of them. Also, new CEOs of charities are often at odds to figure how many of the texts relate to the non-profit sector. This book is less about providing detailed expertise on a specific topic and more about supporting someone new to the role in taking full responsibility for it. It's why we called the book *You're It!* We want it to help a CEO get out of the weeds and think strategically about every aspect of the organization she leads, which is a challenging task at the best of times. We also want the book to help a new CEO make the mental shift to being in charge. This is critical. For someone who has been reporting to a CEO, it can be a significant leap to become one. The truth is that those who make the leap quickly are more likely to be successful: much of the learning is in the doing.

You're It! takes you through the life cycle of being a CEO. It has four sections. The first is about getting ready: deciding whether you're prepared to step into the role; deciphering if the organization is the right choice for you; and using those first few months on the job to set clear plans for yourself and your organization. The second section is about getting the team or the people needed to advance the work. A CEO must take an active role in recruiting and attracting outstanding individuals at all levels, setting the culture and building the support mechanisms that ensure the organization has the skills and commitment necessary to achieve its mission.

The third section deals more concretely with the day-to-day work, from raising and managing money to raising awareness and surrounding the organization with advocates and friends. This is the nitty-gritty that separates mediocre organizations from well-managed ones. The fourth section addresses the difficult question of when it's time to leave the role and take on the next challenge. Someone just starting out may not see the need to read this section. Although it is not something to worry about during the first few months, it will be useful to read it early and remember that the job requires you to leave an organization in better shape than when you started. You are there to guide and steward the organization so that it has a life beyond any one leader.

We did not write *You're It!* with the intention that it be read in one sitting, necessarily. Just as our own conversations have evolved through the years, the book is meant as a companion to be referred to over time. We hope it provides accessible and practical advice that you will adapt to suit your needs, and that will, in turn, translate into achieving your goals and those of your organization. We also hope it serves as a friendly reminder of the importance of your leadership role. A committed, effective leader of integrity can make a huge difference to improving the impact an organization has, and thus an impact on the health and well-being of our society.

So remember *You're It!* and get to work.

PART ONE:

GETTING READY

CHAPTER ONE

MAKING A MOVE

Part A. How Do You Know You Are Ready to Step Up?

People have different motivations for wanting to become a CEO.

Some people, after a few years of managing people, simply crave the challenge of increased responsibility for the strategic direction of an organization. For these people, the desire for continuous learning and professional development will push them toward the role of CEO.

Others have a passion for an issue — such as the environment, poverty, or children's rights — and want to become a CEO so that they can make a greater contribution to the cause that inspires them. In some cases the desire to have a positive influence on a particular issue may have propelled them into a leadership position before they have spent much time thinking about being a leader.

Sometimes individuals are motivated by pure ambition. They want to be the boss. They have a strong entrepreneurial drive and want an organization to move at their speed.

Many people meticulously plan their paths to becoming CEO. For others, the opportunity comes accidentally or much sooner than anticipated; this may be the case if a person's experience is brought to the attention of an organization that is looking for a new leader. In either situation, you will need to determine if you are ready.

Part B. Self-Assessment

A good way to determine your readiness is to critically assess your own skills, both hard (finance, governance) and soft (working with people inside and outside the organization, strategic and business planning). This self-assessment will show the level of competence and experience that you already have, and what areas you need to develop before and during the first few months of taking over as CEO.

Hard-Skills Inventory:

a. **Financial literacy**

Organizations will vary in terms of their accounting-staff support. In fact, the range can be broad, from a member of the board keeping accounts in their spare time, to an elementary staff with a sole bookkeeper, to a competent set of financial staff, to outsourcing of financial management to a professional accounting firm. Regardless of the internal expertise available, a CEO must understand the basics of finance and accounting. Organizations often get in trouble when CEOs don't treat this area seriously or lack appropriate financial literacy to oversee the finances. This task should not be delegated away completely.

There are five key competencies: records keeping and management; controls and auditing; budgeting and monitoring; reporting; and investment management.

1. Records keeping and management: The accounting staff should have a detailed and standard way to keep track of expenditures and revenue (including standard contracts and expense reports) and have the appropriate tools (for example, software, safe storage).

2. Controls and auditing: In order to protect the organization against fraud, the proper controls need to be in place, including clear authorization procedures, monthly reconciliations, cash flow statements, and an annual professional audit. (This can be a full audit, an audit review, or an audit letter.)

3. Budgeting and monitoring: Solid financial management requires detailed and accurate budgets. Good budgets are not about rigid targets; rather, they express the strategic and business objectives of the organization in financial terms. A clear understanding of the costs of the organization's various activities, projects, and operations is required.

4. Reporting: It is essential that a CEO be able to read the basic financial reports, such as a balance sheet or a profit and loss statement, and report on the financial picture of the organization. It is also important to have a good set of regular financial reports. These should track the key factors that contribute to the success of the organization, information that formal audit-based reports don't usually provide. Good financial reports are key communication tools for both internal and external audiences.

5. Investment management: The CEO needs to have some knowledge of the various ways the money of the organization may be invested. A small amount could be managed in a regular bank account or a reserve that is invested in short-term investment instruments. The organization might also have an endowment that requires more sophisticated investment expertise on the board, long-term investment strategies, and the hiring and monitoring of investment advisors. The way an organization manages its money must match its liquidity needs and risk profile.

b.   Governance literacy

Governance literacy is the ability to understand the roles and responsibilities of board members versus those of management. The job of the board is not to manage the organization but to provide the oversight that helps in the proper management of the organization. Good governance requires structures and procedures that ensure accountability and encourage strong performance. Good governance also needs processes and policies to be in place for effective decision-making, including clear reporting procedures, written mandates for the board of directors (with term lengths and a process for evaluating director performance), and regular monitoring and evaluation of management's work.

This is where experience with a board is essential, either as someone who has reported to a board, helped to manage a board's affairs, or served as a volunteer director on a board committee.

Soft-Skills Inventory:

a. **Working with people inside and outside the organization**

At the end of the day, it is the people you are able to engage who determine the success of an organization. This requires knowing which jobs are key, recruiting the right people to fill the positions, and providing those people with the resources and support they need to succeed. Getting people to work well with each other and to share the responsibility for the success of the organization requires solid relationship-management skills.

Organizations also need to develop effective relationships with the outside world. This means understanding whom to engage, and how and when to create effective partnerships and coalitions. In short, you need to be willing and committed to not only working within your organization but also being the ambassador and link to the outside world.

Delegation is a necessary tool of management. A manager, by definition, cannot do every job in an organization, unless it is an organization of one. So assigning the work to others is necessary.

There are many good pieces of advice about how to delegate: make sure the desired outcomes are clear; make sure the standards of performance are clear; make sure the ethical framework is understood; make sure the nature of the delegated tasks matches the talents of the worker to whom the tasks are assigned.

ALAN: I recall an organization a few years ago where the CEO delegated the finance portfolio to the vice president of finance. Whenever finance was discussed at a board meeting, the CEO turned things over to the VP and never had another word to say about financial matters. The CEO would only resume participation when the agenda had moved on to the next item. It ended badly, when the VP made a number of errors of substance and in reporting that the CEO did not catch. In fact, he could not catch them because he had stopped paying attention to finance. He had moved the finance work off his desk and out of his mind, with unhappy results. It took a board intervention to sort out the problems and ultimately undermined the confidence the CEO had enjoyed up to then.

But one of the biggest mistakes a CEO can make is to delegate work without having any basic understanding of the content of that work.

CEOs don't need to know every detail of work being delegated, and probably shouldn't, but they must maintain a basic grasp so they can recognize issues and problems as they arise.

b. Strategic and business planning

To lead an organization, the CEO must be able to clearly articulate the strategic goals for the organization and know how to divide these strategic goals into business activities. A strong strategic plan assesses the current issues facing the organization and articulates a vision that shows where an organization is going over the next few years. It has measurable outcomes so that success is clearly defined. The accompanying business plan should map out, in detail, the path that the organization needs to take to achieve these strategic goals, as well the resources needed to do so.

There are different models and approaches to strategic planning, depending on specifics of the organization (culture, size, governance model). The process of leading different stakeholders through the drafting of strategic and business plans and making sure that people are all on the same page is just as important as the documents that are ultimately produced.

c. Turning ideas into action

The art of "managing" is often described as setting goals, monitoring and reporting results, and managing crises. All of those things are important, it's true, but at the heart of being a manager is something different: it's the ability to turn an idea into actual projects or products. Those who have had experience in creating large projects from scratch have specific skills. They know how to break large pieces of work into smaller, discrete chunks. To effectively manage, one must be able to develop and oversee business processes that break work into pieces small enough that they can be completed by individual workers or teams. This not only ensures that work can be completed in a timely and consistent fashion, but it also makes it easier to produce good quality, to measure results, and to ensure that projects are properly resourced. It is easy to become paralyzed by complicated and complex situations. Leaders need a way to deal with them, an analytical process or framework that makes such situations comprehensible not only to them but also to other people in the organization.

ALAN: A number of years ago, Adam Gopnik, Canadian–American writer, essayist, and commentator, wrote "The Last of the Metrozoids" in the *New Yorker*, about a boys' football team (the Metrozoids) that he and another father started in New York City. They were charged with teaching kids the basic football plays. The other father was a well-known art historian, and he proved adept at teaching kids complicated plays. On the field he would line them up in formation, and then have them walk slowly through a play the first time, with each kid walking his own route. Then they would do it again at a regular walk, and again at a fast walk. Eventually they would be able to run through the play with their own routes well imprinted in their minds. The approach came from the way the art historian taught his students about paintings. He would have them look at a painting and then begin to break it down. Through a series of questions (where are they? what are they doing? who is in the picture? why are they there?), they would disassemble the picture into its component pieces. And then he would have them put it back together, to see what the painter was trying to do. "You break it down, and you build it back up," he said. And that was the way the Metrozoids learned to run football plays.

Leaders can do this with complicated and complex tasks, breaking them down into their component parts and then building them back up with the key actors participating so that everyone can understand what is involved and why each element is there.

Part C. Assessing Your Fit with the Organization

Figuring out what type of organization would best be served by your current abilities and interests is a worthwhile exercise. When deciding whether or not to take up an opportunity to lead an organization, the obvious place to start is with the mission. You need to have an affinity with it. A successful leader is one who believes in the organization's goals, is passionate about advancing the cause, and has the credibility to sell the cause to the outside world.

ALAN: Al Etmanski and Vickie Cammack started the Planned Lifetime Activity Network (PLAN) to help families that had a member living with a disability. PLAN connects the people supporting the person with a disability, including health care providers, educators, and community and institutional workers, as well as other family members, with the goal of providing a more seamless and resilient network of support. From the start Al and Vickie refused to focus on deficits in life but, rather, asked the question "What is a good life?" so that every member of the network could work to provide that for the person at the centre of the network. Al and Vickie kept that mission visible at all times for everyone involved, and this generated successful interventions for people living with disabilities.

Along with the mission, the size and scope of the organization also matter. Is it an organization with five employees or fifty? Does it operate locally or does it have a regional, national, or international mandate?

It used to be that career decisions often made themselves. People worked for the same company most of their lives and advanced through the ranks in an orderly and incremental way, often being tapped on the shoulder when their time for promotion came along. Those days are gone. Most careers involve many different employers and often many different types of work. People move between the private, public, and community sectors, from engineering to finance to management, and from large to small organizations and possibly back again. It is imperative to ensure that your work choices match your talents, desire, and ambition, and to focus on that alignment.

But it is also important to be sure you take into account the needs and interests of the employer. There are many stories of people who have been offered a promotion but turned it down (perhaps it involved moving to another city or leaving a comfort zone), only to find their career path taking a downward, or outward, turn.

> **ALAN:** A friend of mine turned down a promotion in another city only to find himself offered a severance package a year later, which he had to accept. The result was a loss of half a decade of peak-earning years until he finally found his way back into the industry in a much more junior position. He had never really considered that his employers had their own interest in his career, and when they became misaligned, they took what they considered the necessary steps.

The culture of the organization and the stage of development of the organization are also important in determining fit. Is the organization in trouble and in need of major restructuring? If so, the board may be looking for a turnaround leader who will need to assess the problems and quickly create a short-term plan to renew the organization. Turnaround leaders are able to manage and resolve crises, can manage a high level of stress, and are able to inspire confidence. They are efficient and expeditious problem solvers who are comfortable with conflict and adversity, and they often have a thick skin. Turnaround organizations need a higher-than-average level of hands-on management for an intensive amount of time.

Is the organization in its early stages of development or in need of a boost? An organization looking for an entrepreneurial leader needs someone to help generate ideas. The quintessential quality of entrepreneurial leaders is creativity. They consistently see new opportunities that no one else has noticed. They focus on creating value by finding better ways of doing things and with lower costs. They enjoy taking risks — venturing into unknown territory, breaking rules, and going against the status quo. Often, organizations that are just starting out have limited resources; the qualities of an entrepreneurial leader are essential to the development of this kind of organization.

Is the organization well-established and successful and looking for a steady managerial leader? In this case, the organization will likely have solid structures in place, and it needs someone who is able to promote and advance the organization's goals within an established vision. Managerial leaders are strong at consensus-building, willing to spend the time necessary to learn about the history and culture of a place, and able to adapt to it. They are relationship-oriented. They make sure they have good people in place with the proper resources. They are able to direct program improvements and quality control, and advance the cause without looking like they are rocking the boat.

Knowing your own skills, strengths, and weaknesses at the outset is therefore extremely important. If your skills are fundamentally entrepreneurial in nature, you probably aren't going to enjoy a turnaround situation and you might feel stifled at an organization that is already well-established. Conversely, if your style is that of a steady managerial leader, you might want to think twice before stepping on the roller coaster of a recent start-up. You must be hard-nosed and honest about this self-assessment. If you believe that you have the skills, experience, and interest to be all of the aforementioned types of leader, well, you may just be too delusional to hold the post and be an effective leader.

ALAN: When you are thinking about moving up the ladder, be sure you are moving to a job you can succeed at. I have a personal process that I undertake from time to time, every few years at least, where I make four lists: things I am good at; things I am not good at; things I like to do; and things I don't like to do. For example, I am not interested in details, and I don't like making cold calls on the telephone. Some of the things I'm good at, like chairing committees, I don't like very much. When I am faced with an opportunity, I see how it matches up with those lists. The best situation, of course, is matching things you are good at and things that you like. But when you have a job opportunity, it is good to have an analytical framework, even a simple one like mine, to hold it up against as an indication of whether it might be the right job or the wrong job for you.

Things I'm Good At
Things I'm not Good At
Things I like to do
Things I dont like to do

The Four Lists	
Things I am GOOD at	Things I LIKE to do
Things I am NOT GOOD at	Things I DON'T LIKE to do

You should also be comfortable with the salary. Often, people taking on their first leadership position will be quite modest with their salary request and accept a salary that is too low. They undervalue their own skills and experiences, and they are so happy to have been picked that they undersell themselves. It is your responsibility to get a strong sense of the organization's finances and the comparable salary range for the position, and to know if an organization is able to meet your salary expectations. If so, you must make your case to the organization. Your ability to advocate for your own interests in a fair and firm manner is often seen as an indicator of how effectively you will be able to advocate for the organization. In your contract of employment, you should also negotiate the terms of separation with fair terms of notice and severance, in order to make your eventual departure orderly.

Part D. Preparing for the Interview Process

When you reach the stage of considering leading a specific organization, you need to do your due diligence. You may want to start by undertaking an environmental scan to learn where the organization sits in its competitive environment. Your research should uncover who else is operating in the sector, how the organization is perceived, and what the organization's strengths and weaknesses are according to the outside world. You should also develop a strong sense of the various stakeholders and key players involved in the organization. Who will have the final say on crucial decisions? To whom does the current CEO listen? Who has special powers outside of their formal role? Who needs to be treated differently? Who are the key donors? Is the founder involved? Within any organization there are people with particular, entrenched interests. A few of these people hold trump cards. The CEO needs to know who holds them and what they are. There may be certain challenges that you think you are up to, but you should be paying careful attention to warning signs that an organization is not healthy or not really interested in hiring the type of CEO you are going to be.

In your preliminary environmental scan and research, you will identify gaps in your knowledge that will form the basis of the questions you will ask in the interview. First-time CEOs tend to be shy in their approach to the interview process, wanting to prove that they can do the job. Interviewing for a CEO position must be a two-way conversation. The organization is interviewing to determine if the candidate is suitable, but as the potential CEO, you must be strategic and use the interview to learn if the organization is one you want to lead.

> **FRANCA:** I was young, I wanted the job, and I thought I knew what the current challenges of the organization were. Instead, in the first few months I spent considerable time discovering a different set of challenges, including an impending deficit that had not been clear to me at the beginning. The problem was that I had not spent enough time during the interview process asking questions. I would not do that again. It's not that the answers would have discouraged me from taking on the job, but if I had asked better questions, I would have been more clear about what I was taking on.

After the interview(s), there should be no question about the type of leader the organization is looking for, what its current challenges are, what its financial situation is, and what its short- and long-term objectives are. You should ask why the previous CEO is leaving, whether the organization is looking for similar or different traits in their new CEO, and what the reasoning is behind that. Financial clarity is essential. No organization is going to be able to provide a new CEO with perfect financial security and five years' worth of money in the bank, but a prospective CEO has to know what they would have to work with.

Leadership controls

What kind of leader are you looking for?

Summary

The process of being hired will tell you a lot about the culture of the organization. Are they prepared to answer questions? Are they transparent or are they unable to provide the information you are asking for? Which person(s) will actually be making the hiring decision? Are there clear decision-making processes in place? Do the interviewers present a cohesive vision or do they have different ways of talking about the organization's mission? Do they have a strong sense of the challenges and opportunities? Is the board looking for a visionary to help set the course or an administrator to facilitate their work? Are they familiar with the organization's current financial information? Are they willing to share the latest financial statements? If, after a long interview process, you are not getting direct answers to your questions, you might need to rethink if this is the organization for you.

TIPS AND RESOURCES --------------------------------

1. Build your online profile. LinkedIn, for example, is today's CV and a go-to resource for hiring managers. Make sure your profile is accurate and up to date. If you are using social media tools such as Twitter or Facebook, make sure the content is consistent with what you would like a potential employer to see and know about you.

2. Find a reason to say yes. Leaping into your first role as leader is never going to feel comfortable or secure. It is a huge responsibility, and there will always be reasons to say no. Don't let these stop you from making a positive contribution to your community. If the opportunity is right, step up to the plate.

3. It is a myth that leaders have to be extroverts. Susan Cain's *Quiet: The Power of Introverts in a World That Can't Stop Talking* (Crown Publishing Group, 2012) is a great book that encourages introverts to take on leadership roles. Introverts make some of the best leaders as they tend to be good listeners. That said, if you are an introvert, you'll need to figure out how to be situationally extroverted because the role will require it.

Best leaders are good listeners

(Taking Notes

* OCIO transition

* Program Renewal Launches

* Early Feedback from my colleagues

* Governance question, thought to Sandy's role

* First question: why was I chosen Better or Different?

CHAPTER TWO

GETTING THE JOB AND GETTING STARTED

Congratulations! You got the job! Now, what do you do? First, avoid the temptation to make promises and set strategic goals in the first few weeks. This is a common impulse for new leaders, especially first-time CEOs with heroic notions. They run the risk of setting expectations that are too high, making promises that are unrealistic, or acting before thoroughly understanding the organization. Equally troubling, they miss the opportunity that a CEO only truly has in the first few weeks on the job — to get honest and direct feedback from the organization's stakeholders. Once you are fully integrated in the organization, these stakeholders may not be as willing or able to openly share their thoughts with you.

Part A. The First Meeting with the Board Chair

As soon as you have accepted the position, you should plan to have a conversation with the person responsible for good

29

governance who sets the tone for the board — the board chair. A key question to ask is why you were chosen over the other candidates who were interviewed for the position. We usually assume that we were picked because we were better than the other candidates, but it may be that we were just different. It is useful to understand that difference, so ask. First-time CEOs, in particular, may feel too awkward or too grateful for having been chosen to ask the question directly.

> **FRANCA:** I definitely made this mistake when I was offered the job at the Loran Scholars Foundation. I was so excited to be given the opportunity that I never asked our chairman these questions. I found out months into the job about the other candidates, and I must admit that by that time it was not that useful. For example, I learned in an indirect way that one of the candidates became one of my board directors. This person had extensive fundraising experience, which the board thought I lacked. I had learned in a more painful indirect way what the expectations were. I should have asked our chairman why *I* was chosen, and what the other candidates had that I lacked.

Usually a search committee selects a candidate for the CEO role because the committee believes that the individual will be able to provide the type of leadership the organization needs at that moment in time. In other words, it is valuable to know what kind of leader the search committee expects you to be. Equally interesting is to find out what kind of leaders the organization did *not* choose. Were the other candidates perceived as being too conventional? Too risky? Or did they not demonstrate enough of a vision? You know this from hiring your own staff. You do not necessarily hire the candidate with the best resume, but the person you think best fits the specific job requirements.

Another useful piece of information is why the previous CEO left the organization. Is your hiring a distancing from the past, or is there an expectation that you will continue the work of your predecessor? Is the organization hoping to enhance and maintain the same course of action, or does it see this as an opportunity for a considerable shift from the status quo? What was the relationship like between the CEO and the board, and between the CEO and board chair?

At this first meeting with the board chair, it is also helpful to ask again some of the questions you posed during the interview process. Ask the chair to elaborate on a few of the answers, and address any issues that were too sensitive to deal with during the interview. You will want to ask, again, who will have the final say on important organizational decisions, and who the most influential stakeholders and donors are. Who holds the trump cards?

At this meeting, you may also want to ask the chair about the background of the board directors and his or her thoughts on their performance. You want to know what are the two or three key issues that the board is dealing with, and which critical issues need to be addressed immediately.

You may also want to let your board chair know of your intention to consult stakeholders and ask who, in his or her opinion, the key individuals to meet with are and why. You should also set a regular meeting time with the chair in the next few months to ensure you get to know each other and to keep him or her informed of your initial plans.

Part B. Consulting Stakeholders

For the first thirty to forty days, it is a good idea to meet with the key stakeholders of the organization: past board chairs, key donors or investors, and key volunteers. The list will most likely evolve as you speak with people. The chair will probably give you names at your initial meeting, and those individuals will in turn suggest other people. The list should include stakeholders who have not always been happy with the work of the organization, have a critical opinion, and are willing to share this with you.

The purpose of these conversations is to pose the question, "What does success for the organization look like?" The research and preparation you did for the job interview should have resulted in a detailed environmental scan and a clear understanding of how the organization fits into this larger picture. This information is a good foundation for you to build on as you draft questions for the stakeholder meetings. Before visiting with someone, do your homework. Although individuals will not expect a new CEO to have developed a plan for the organization at this point, they will expect you to know the contributions they have made and the roles they have played in the history of the organization. They will also expect to see that you are committed to the mission of the organization.

Overall, these conversations will be listening exercises. The old adage that you have two ears and one mouth and should use them in that proportion applies. This is an opportunity to hear people articulate the vision of the organization and why they have decided to support it. This is also an opportunity to have them express some of their concerns and frustrations. You should be clear with people about this objective when you set up the meetings. The message is that, as you are starting your job, you want to benefit from the knowledge of the individuals who have been committed to the work of the organization. These visits are fact-finding expeditions.

You are there to hear their thoughts, not to tell them where the organization will go under your leadership. It will be tempting to address any concerns they may have with promises about what you will be able to accomplish for the organization and how you will bring the organization to the promised land. Resist the temptation to get out there and make promises before you know you are able to keep them. A new leader needs time to form her vision of what success looks like, independent from the need to please or appease one or two individuals. Thank people for sharing their thoughts and remind them (and yourself) how useful it is to have the information. But even in the face of contentious feedback, don't engage in an argument. There will be opportunities for you to share your vision. The first few months in

Adage: Two ears and one mouth and we should use them in that proportion.

an organization is the only time that you can enjoy being the new person around, so sit back and listen.

Here are a few key questions to guide these conversations:

- What is the basic business of the organization? And what are the key pillars of the work?
- Are there areas of support for the organization that have gone untapped? What are the missed opportunities? And what would the organization have to do to fully take advantage of these opportunities?
- What is done well and what is not done well by the organization?
- What are the challenges or threats facing the organization and why?
- If they were the new CEO, what would they focus on first?
- What do they consider the strengths and weakness of the management team? The point with this last question is not to conduct a performance appraisal. You will conduct your own internal evaluation of the team, which will be more accurate. It is useful to get external feedback to screen for any inconsistencies between internal and external perceptions. For example, a staff member might be highly disruptive or inefficient internally, but the stakeholders are quick to praise him or her, or vice versa.

This consultation process will result in a fuller, more detailed picture of the organization. It is highly likely that you will get different ideas of the key drivers of the organization.

A leader needs to learn the different perspectives so he or she can judge what needs to be pulled together, what needs to be clarified, and what ambiguity needs to be left alone. The process will most likely provide you with an understanding of what the organization values. It will also give you a good sense of the culture of the place and how decisions are made.

These conversations are also a great way of getting to know the key stakeholders. As you develop the vision for the organization going forward, you will have a clear idea of who will need to be brought on board and who will be your strongest supporters. It will help you to identify potential relationship pitfalls so that you can devise a way to address them.

ALAN: Murray Ross, the first president of York University, once told me, "you can never go wrong listening to what people have to say." I've found that to be sound advice. But you also need to develop some defensive tactics when the conversation turns into a rant, slander, or character assassination. In this consultation phase, where confrontation would be gratuitous at best, it would be good to claim "overload" and ask if the rant or other unpleasantries might be put over to a subsequent discussion. That discussion might never need to occur.

Since the purpose of this consultation is to get a good read of the organization, at some point it will become clear that the returns are no longer there and that you have the information you need. Put an end to it and start planning.

As you progress through the planning stages, you may want to go back to a number of the individuals with whom you met. Once you have put together your vision, you will want to ask a few of the people you initially consulted for their help in refining and implementing this vision. This is an opportunity to establish some key allies of your own.

Part C. Confirm Your Fit

As you are doing this information-gathering work, you may come to find that things may not have been fully disclosed; that something happened that materially altered the conditions of the work; or that you failed to do your due diligence. You will quickly have to assess whether you can be an effective leader in this environment. Face up to it sooner than later and be realistic. If the changes are material enough that they make you question your ability to do the job, or that they alter the fit of your skills to the job, then it is best to own up to it fast.

Of course, the situation has to be materially different from what you've been given to understand, not just annoying or hard. The organization has invested time and resources in its search for you. You have a responsibility to take this seriously and do your homework before the job is offered and accepted. Once you're the leader, you can't back away simply because things have gotten difficult.

Summary

The first few months as the CEO are particularly important and can help you set a tone with the people inside and outside the organization. Spend most of your time listening to your stakeholders and understanding clearly why you have been chosen to lead the organization. Resist the temptation to go with the tide, and don't allow yourself to make any promises until you are well-grounded in what the organization needs.

TIPS AND RESOURCES ------------------------------

1. Get a theme song in your head: It could be Ani DiFranco's "Smile Pretty and Watch Your Back," U2's "Beautiful Day," Carl Orff's "O Fortuna," or Ennio Morricone's "The Ecstasy of Gold." In those early days, when things are coming at you quickly, having a few notes in your head will bring you back to yourself and the energy, positivity, boldness, and patience you require.

2. *Act Like a Leader, Think Like a Leader* by Herminia Ibarra (Harvard Business Review Press, 2015) is a fantastic read that argues that the best way to grow and develop as a leader is by action and by experience, not by introspection. For a first-time leader or someone changing leadership roles, it's a wonderful, practical

reminder that at some point you need to stop thinking and start doing.

3. Set your priorities and boundaries. As you become familiar with the expectations and workplace culture, think about what you need to do to maintain your health and a good home–work balance. The role of a CEO does not typically end at 5:00 p.m. How will you make time for personal relationships? Will you establish a regular exercise schedule? Setting positive habits from the beginning will enhance your role in both your professional and personal lives.

CHAPTER THREE

CRAFTING THE VISION

If you are leading an organization, you probably believe in its work or mission. Whether it is designing software, awarding scholarships, providing shelter to homeless people, or protecting the environment, you are clear on what the organization's purpose is. Often, the factors that will help the organization achieve that goal are less obvious. In other words, what is the core business for the organization? As a new CEO, you must take some time to figure this out. If you don't, your operations can go spinning out in all directions very quickly. Defining your core business is not always simple, but once articulated, it results in a clear vision.

We are using the term "vision" in a very different way than people are accustomed to using it. For most organizations, a vision is a lofty, often unattainable statement. In fact, it has become *de rigueur* for organizations to plan weekend-long board and staff retreats and spend resources coming up with lofty visions such as "eradicating poverty" or "developing a sustainable world." In addition, vision statements are often followed by an equally generic list of values such as "we will act with honesty," "we will operate at the highest ethical standards," "we will be entrepreneurial." The warning note with this approach is that it can lead to non-specific or unrealistic statements that leave management with little guide for decision-making or accountability.

For us, "vision" refers to a set of practical statements that identify the organization's core business and are used to guide the strategic decisions of the organization. Each individual statement identifies a key driver of the organization's work. These statements are practical enough that management and board could have a healthy debate on whether they have identified the right ones. These drivers collectively provide a clear picture of what you, as a leader, need to focus on to ensure the success of your organization. Taking the time to define the key drivers early on in the job is an indispensable first step.

Part A. The Value of the Key Drivers: Organizational Examples

Two or three key drivers are at the root of most organizations' work. A good manager must be able to identify them and state them simply and concretely.

Clearly articulated drivers will provide leaders with a solid way of testing whether new ideas fit the purpose of the organization. Since not everything is equally important, these drivers will help you to focus on the priorities of the organization. In a profit-making organization, the drivers must identify what makes the business more profitable and distinctive in the marketplace.

> **ALAN:** I remember some years ago walking into the office of the new CEO of Blacks Photo Corporation. He had a number of large sheets of paper taped to the walls of the office. He had mapped out the various products and business processes trying to identify the core of the business. He came up with two key drivers: providing high quality photo finishing and running a strong marketing program. Once he identified the drivers, it became quite obvious to him that the other stuff, such as the delivery process to the stores, was secondary and could be outsourced.

For a non-profit organization, articulating the drivers can at times be a little trickier. When you manage an organization based on the generosity of donors or government resources, for example, it can be quite easy to start to let the funding sources guide the business decisions and divert the mission of the organization. It becomes about "what can we get money to do?" as opposed to "what do we need to do?" A new CEO could suddenly find that the organization is doing all kinds of things it should not be doing. Teasing out what is core to the work may at times be a matter of survival.

FRANCA: I faced a critical decision in my first few months on the job with the Loran Scholars Foundation with regard to budget cuts. The organization was facing a deficit, and we needed to make tough cuts. I needed to have a clear idea of what was core to our work. I identified three key drivers: a selection system aimed at finding unconventional students with potential for leadership; a stewardship program that provides scholars with opportunities to realize this potential; and a fundraising program that ensures renewed and diversified revenue sources. Once I had done that, it became obvious that we could not afford to reduce the travel budget to visit regional committees in any meaningful way as our regional selection system is a key driver. But I could reduce costs by outsourcing our bookkeeping, our tech support, some of our communications activities, and our events planning.

Part B. Deciding on the Key Drivers

Unless you are the CEO of a start-up, in most cases you are coming into an inherited situation. This means that it can often be easier to avoid articulating the key drivers. You may have many people willing to tell you what you should definitely *not* do. For example, don't touch the bookkeeper that has been with the organization for fifteen years, and make sure to keep running the fundraising gala that has been going since we started. People are used to doing what they have been doing. Articulating the key drivers can make the need for certain changes painfully obvious. Resistance by some is inevitable, but the cost of not clarifying the core business is too great to put off this exercise.

Before drafting the key drivers, of course, you want to make sure you have a comprehensive understanding of the organization. Start by breaking down the work and identifying the various programs, processes, and products of the organization. The next step is to look at the full picture and figure out what the business couldn't do without by separating the things you *need to have* to run the business from the *nice to have*. This is a subtle but essential difference that requires vigorous testing. You are prioritizing the organization's needs.

The key roadblock in articulating the drivers is often one's own resistance to making decisions for fear of potential negative consequences. Figure out what is behind the resistance. For example, is a board director or a donor connected to the thing that you know needs to change? Is a popular or powerful staff member running a part of the operation that may be expendable? Make plans that will minimize the negative reactions, as noted previously, but don't let this stop you from being clear on what your core business is.

ALAN: I joined the board of a venerable national organization in the mid-90s and realized that the institute had an extensive news-clipping service. It was something they had been doing for the last seventy years, and they had developed quite an extensive clippings library. In fact, it was the best in the country. For an organization with limited resources in the Internet age with its free, accessible media, it was quite apparent to me that this was an area that needed to change. The problem was that there was a woman who had been running this service for the last twenty years, and no one wanted to eliminate her position. It took three years to finally stop this practice. I remember I finally spoke with her and asked how she would feel if we gave her a pension that was equivalent to working at the institute for another three years. She said she would take it in a minute.

Part C. Organizing the Work Around the Drivers

Once you have the drivers clearly articulated, start to embed them into all aspects of the organization. A good next step is to break down the budget in terms of these drivers to see what resources are going into each major task. This provides a good tool for evaluating the current situation and ensures that the appropriate resources are marshalled in support of the drivers, rather than spread thinly and evenly everywhere. As a leader where are you focusing your time and that of your team? What resources are being poorly spent? How many resources are you allocating to the top drivers of the organization?

After you have broken down what the organization is currently doing, the next step is to set goals for improving performance on the drivers. What needs to change to make a greater impact? What works perfectly and should not be changed? Who needs to be involved to achieve the goals? What needs to happen first? What team do you need? Who are the most vital new recruits? For example, depending on the organization, it might be the chief information officer or chief technology officer or it could be front line workers or nurses.

ALAN: For the University of Toronto, one of the most vital recruits for a CEO is the vice president in charge of fundraising. This research-intensive public institution has arguably three key drivers: attracting top faculty and their research funding; producing world-class research in a broad range of disciplines; and raising a growing and diversified stream of revenue. That the latter is a key driver was never clearer than during Robert Prichard's term as president (1990–2000). During his tenure, he launched the most aggressive university fundraising campaign in Canada. It is no surprise, then, that the man heading the campaign was reportedly paid more than anyone at the university.

By letting the drivers guide the goal setting process, work plans evolve quite naturally, and they form concrete strategic and business plans for the organization whose progress and activities will be quite straightforward to measure. That said, even if an idea sounds like it fits with your drivers, it must still be tested.

> **ALAN**: I was once associated with a high-end hotel, and they were in the process of organizing a major renovation of their guest rooms. A key driver was securing repeat business from wealthy clients who enjoyed luxury. They had a designer come in to give advice to the managing director. The designer suggested that the hotel use expensive wallpaper by Laura Ashley. The argument was that this luxurious touch would attract the high-end clients. Before going ahead, we decided to test whether this expenditure was worth it and I remember being pleasantly surprised by what we found. We talked with consultants in the hotel industry who test and evaluate the various strategies that can be engaged to satisfy customers and make them want to return. These experts made it quite clear that we could achieve the same result by simply leaving two chocolate truffles on the pillows.

You should also consider organizing management reports to the board and stakeholders by the key drivers. All activities of the organization can then be reviewed quarterly to see how they fit (or don't fit) the key drivers. It helps the board remain focused on the vision. This will often provide a transparent reason to say no to "helpful" advice you might get as a new CEO, especially around the board table or from well-intentioned donors.

> **FRANCA:** At the Loran Scholars Foundation, two of our key drivers are our extensive selection process involving hundreds of trained volunteers across Canada, and a scholars' stewardship program which includes mentorship, summer internships, and peer support aimed at maximizing the scholars' potential. We organize our management report to the board by these drivers. Our core work must fit in one of those two drivers; if not, it is a good indicator that we may be off mission.

In short, the drivers make the entire organization more manageable and understandable. They take the ambiguity out of strategic decision-making and provide guidance to the staff on their daily activities, but they cannot be seen as static. As CEO it is your job to keep yourself up to date and to be sensitive to any changes in your market or operating environment. Although you might rely on key people to help you, such as the fundraiser to let you know of changes in the fundraising community, or your operations or finance person to let you know of any shifts in the regulatory environment, as

Network of people w skills + experience in regulation + sector affairs Margaret, Maureen, Robin, etc.

CEO you are ultimately responsible to make sure the organization is responding adequately and in a timely fashion.

Summary

The CEO should always be aware of the key drivers: their state of play and how they are operating in the larger context. Conditions can and will change, and you need to be ready to adjust what you do and how you do it. The organization and its leadership should have enough flexibility to adapt and adjust. It is not appropriate to say that the current business plan or the current budget does not allow you to look at something, or that you'll wait until next year. Change the plans or the budget when you need to change them. If there is a need to reconsider the drivers, don't wait or it might be too late.

TIPS AND RESOURCES ------------------------------

1. Peter Drucker's *Managing the Non-profit Organization: Principles and Practices* (HarperBusiness, 1992) is a must-read classic. It is written on the premise that non-profits are more complex to manage because they don't have the single purpose of profit. It will help you think through what your organization's purpose is and how important it is to organize the work around it.

2. Nick Saul's chapter "Reimagining Your Organization" in *Five Good Ideas: Practical Strategies for Non-Profit Success* (Coach House Books, 2011) tells the story of how he reimagined The Stop from a food bank to an organization with a more comprehensive and successful approach to food security. He provides practical advice on what matters the most when you lead these types of changes.

3. Choose your tools. There are many tools that will help you work through your thoughts and explore possibilities as you craft your vision. Depending on how you work best, you might consider online mind mapping software such as MindMeister (www.mindmeister.com), or you may prefer a flipchart with multicoloured markers. Either way, exploring possibilities from different angles will only enrich your vision.

Watch Closely
+
Listen Intently

CHAPTER FOUR

MAKING PLANS

Once you have a comprehensive understanding of the key drivers of the organization, you are ready to develop strategic and business plans. Good plans are used to galvanize your team to reach agreed-upon and measurable goals. Plans outline future growth and development by prioritizing an organization's work for the next three to five years. There is certainly no shortage of resources regarding the preparation of strategic plans, and it's not a bad idea to familiarize yourself with the literature in this area if you're about to start a planning exercise. The rest of this chapter is focused less on the nuts and bolts of plan-making than it is with the *process* of preparing a good plan and, in particular, the way to ensure that your plans get the necessary buy-in throughout your organization.

There is a three-level hierarchy of plans that every organization needs.

- The **Strategic Plan** identifies key corporate priorities and sets broad organizational objectives.
- The **Operating/Business Plan** defines the tactics that the organization will pursue in attempting to meet the key objectives set out in the strategic plan.

- The **Sub-Operating/Sectional Plans** provide the specifics on how the work will be done. This last level is the one that lets team leaders (or, in a smaller office, individual employees) know what they should be doing, and what they will be held accountable for.

Plan	Sets	Who Should Write It	Who Approves It
Strategic	Overall vision and strategy	CEO	Board
Operating/ Business	Achievable goals	CEO with Staff	CEO (given to board for information)
Sub-Operating/ Sectional	Specific activities to be pursued by individual units or employees	Staff	Senior Staff responsible for implementing the work

Part A. The Strategic Plan

A strategic plan is, in essence, a collection of a few key statements about what the organization is going to prioritize for the next few years. Some organizations redo their plans every couple of years, sometimes spending months and months undertaking elaborate consultation processes that culminate in weekend-long board retreats. While consulting with your stakeholders is often useful, good strategy isn't episodic. The process of scanning the environment and making necessary adjustments to goals is something you should be doing on a regular basis. All organizations should have built-in feedback loops so that top management is aware at all times of where its donors, clients, staff, and stakeholders stand. When this is the case, there is no need to engage in a formal consultation process to determine what improvements and changes you need to make; you see them as they emerge and adjust accordingly.

A strategic planning process can be more helpful in determining priorities among goals rather than in setting them. Linking the strategic plan with sub-operating or sectional plan is also helpful in identifying how you will measure success, allocate the resources, and set the schedules for achieving goals.

Some people may argue that the principles of good governance dictate that the board develops the strategic plan and then the CEO implements it. In reality, as CEO, you need to take full charge of drafting a strategic plan to be approved by the board. The board is ultimately responsible for ensuring it is the right plan for the organization and for overseeing its implementation, but as the day-to-day manager of the organization, you need to be providing the options and possibilities for the strategic direction.

Boards of directors are usually diverse collections of individuals with different personal strengths and interests. The primary job of boards is to hire the right CEO and ensure that the organization maintains realistic standards of performance. It is also their job to ensure that the organization has a strategic plan that is doable, desirable, and measurable. It is not their job to come up with the plan in the first place.

As a CEO, *you* are the full-time employee whose responsibility it is to provide the strategic direction for the organization. Board and staff members should not be asked to spend large amounts of time on this process; their talents are needed elsewhere. Remember that no one likes surprises; as CEO, you need to be constantly taking the pulse of your board, staff, and stakeholders and assessing how they see the world evolving. One of your main jobs is to make sure everyone stays focused on getting things done and accomplishing the mission. One way to do this is to assume the responsibility of setting the strategic direction yourself.

> **FRANCA**: Before I use a board member's time, I assess whether this the best use of the talent they have to offer. Often I would rather they make five phone calls to potential donors or send five letters of introduction to potential new friends, rather than spend the same amount of time sitting through another committee meeting. I only get so much of someone's time. I want to make sure it is used to advance our mission.

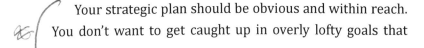

Your strategic plan should be obvious and within reach. You don't want to get caught up in overly lofty goals that aren't going to translate to practical plans. The heart of any strategic plan will lie in the key drivers discussed in the previous chapter. If you understand those and can enunciate them clearly, then the strategic plan shouldn't represent any dramatic shift. This means that you should not need to bring in outside consultants to prepare a plan for you. After all, why ask a stranger to tell you what's best for your organization? As the CEO, it is your job to have answers to that question by being aware of the needs of your board, staff, clients, and stakeholders. Although there may be limited and specific reasons to seek outside advice on certain specific aspects of planning, as the CEO you should be the one driving the process at all times. You are not a passenger.

> **ALAN:** One of the biggest mistakes I've seen — and I must say that I see this mostly on corporate boards I have sat on — is the tendency to take time out from the work to develop a strategic plan. As a result, the costs of developing the strategic plan become astronomical. When you add up the costs of staff time, consultants, and retreats, not to mention opportunity cost, it can become very expensive.

The exception to this rule is if an organization is going through some kind of radical change. If it is in reinvention mode, or in a turnaround situation, there might be cause to take additional time to rethink the business or to get some specific expertise to inform the discussion.

> **ALAN:** At the Tides Canada Foundation, after six years of robust start-up, we decided to put a management structure around the business we'd developed and focus on the strongest elements to achieve our mission and carry us into the future. Because so many board and staff members had been closely engaged in the first stage of Tides, we decided to engage a consultant to challenge us to break out of our own conception of Tides business and its future.

A good place to start any planning process is simply to have informal chats with a few of the key directors and staff members. Let them know that you are developing a strategic plan, and provide them with some broad strokes of your own thinking. This will give you an opportunity to gauge initial reactions to your ideas. Ask if there is anything you should be thinking about in particular, any big concerns that people have regarding the next three to five years. These informal chats will provide you with insight into their ideas about the direction of the organization, give you a number of solid ideas, and clarify who will be supportive and who will need to be brought along.

It is a good idea at this stage to avoid formal strategic planning meetings so as not to commit to including anything specific in the plan before you have had a chance to think thoroughly and holistically about it. All you need at this point in the process is some input. Once you complete this initial phase, you should get down to writing the first draft of the plan and identify the three or four key goals in broad terms. You want to go back to the key decision-makers and show them this draft. Then you can start dealing with any fundamental disagreements.

Remember that keeping the board informed is your responsibility. You do not want to surprise them with any major change of direction or new program. You want to test ideas with board members and have an opportunity to discuss your ideas one-on-one with both your directors and your key staff members.

FRANCA: I find the conversations with board, staff, and stakeholders to be the most vital part of drafting a strategic plan, not for brainstorming but for relationship management. Using the strategic planning process as an opportunity to have one-on-one conversations with the people surrounding the Loran Scholars Foundation allows me a touch point where I can learn about them as individuals and the strengths and talents they can contribute as well as provide them with an update, ask for input, or demystify any misconceptions.

Boards don't like surprises, but many a CEO has been bewildered when she has triumphantly tabled a fully formed plan only to have a number of board members rebel.

Eventually the plan may be adopted with few changes, but surprised and disgruntled board members can delay approval and cause more work. "No surprises" is a good thing to keep in mind.

By the time you take the draft plan to the board, it should be quite familiar to people around the table. Make sure that the plan is discussed as part of a regular meeting of the board. Don't fetishize strategy by making it the subject of a retreat or a special meeting; discussing a strategic plan should simply be considered regular board business. You should plan to have a good discussion on these initial broad strokes, and you should expect to make some revisions based on the group discussion. At the next board meeting, the strategic plan should be brought back for final approval, alongside the business plan.

Part B. The Business Plan

Once you have a first draft of the strategic plan, you will want to develop the business plan that identifies the tactics on how you will accomplish the goals outlined. Essentially, you will need to take the strategic plan, break it down, and then build it back up. For this you need to involve your staff and, together, identify the specific tasks, the timing, and the resources needed, as well the feedback loops that will measure how you are doing. If the strategic plan is about what you are going to do (for example, diversify and increase revenue), the business plan is about how you are going to do it (for example, launch a major gift campaign that will add

Tasks Timing Resources Measures

20% to the revenue). There are various ways you can go about meeting the target, but the most likely road to success is one rooted in the strengths and opportunities of your organization. As a result, you will set the course by identifying what you will and will *not* do: for example, launching an annual major gift fundraising campaign instead of running an event; or running a grassroots direct-mail campaign versus a large-scope endowment drive; building an entrepreneurial venture rather than a capital campaign. All of these might be viable options, but determining which to choose is dependent on the organization's mission, resources available, and other factors.

The business plan is the place to look to determine if an organization is committed to achieving its strategic objectives. If, for example, a strategic goal is to increase public awareness of an issue or problem, you'd want to see that staff and resources are allocated to communications. If the goal is to engage volunteers in mentoring youth or artists, then there should be a well-supported plan for the recruitment, training, scheduling, and monitoring of the mentors. You want to test if the funds are appropriately allocated. If something doesn't appear in the budget, it means it isn't important to the organization.

Part C. Sub-Operating/Sectional Plans

The sub-operating plans will provide you with the nuts and bolts of what tasks are in each part of the operation, when they will be rolled out and completed, how much each will

[handwritten margin note: A few key statements about what we are going to prioritize over a period of time.]

[handwritten bottom note: Strategic Plan: what you are going to do / Business Plan: How you are going to do it (tasks, timing, resources)]

cost, who will be in charge and involved, and how it will be evaluated along the way. The CEO needs to approve these plans, but much of this needs to be delegated. Your staff must provide you with detailed sectional plans for their areas, such as fundraising or communications. At this stage you may be able to see if you have overextended your commitments. If so, this is the time to make some choices between competing priorities.

> **FRANCA**: At the Loran Scholars Foundation, a strategic goal at one point was to increase the number of qualified finalists. Two tactics we decided on were adding to the number of committees in the regions and increasing training and evaluation of their members. The sub-operating plans addressed questions such as how many and which committees needed to be added and when. We decided on the additional resources, the implications for human resources, and the feedback loops and evaluation measures. We looked at our current business structures and determined the impact on administration, travel schedules, training modules, volunteer recruitment, and evaluation process.

Both the business plan and sub-operating plans should include budgets outlining the short- and long-term financial implications of each tactic. You will need to look not just at the numbers for the next twelve months, but also at the projections for the next four years. This will provide an understanding of where you are heading based on the assumptions embedded in the plans. A new idea might not result in a substantial increase in the first year, but by the time it is rolled out, the idea may cost more than revenue projections can handle.

When you are facing uncertainty, develop scenarios. You may decide that you want to grow the revenue by 20%, but what will happen if you don't? What would the impact on the organization be if you grew 10% or 30%? It will help to have a few scenarios and contingency plans so that you can be bold in your ambition without putting the organization at high risk. Knowing what alternative scenarios look like will make mid-course adjustments easier.

The business plan should be flexible enough to adapt to changes in the marketplace. If you are launching a pilot program that turns out not to show the expected results, you want to be able to adapt and change course. If the market crashes or a key donor decides to stop funding you, you will probably have to change your priorities.

The plans should be concise and written in everyday language, without acronyms or archaic language. You want to be able to tell people what your plans are for the organization within a few minutes; if you need a ten-page PowerPoint presentation to explain it, you need to go back to the drawing board.

It may be useful to consider what kind of contribution you would like to make to, for example, public policy or research. Understandably, organizations with limited resources often become inward-looking. This planning process should be used as an opportunity to think about how your own learning could serve the larger public good. For example, have you figured out a way to address child poverty in your community that could be scaled up by sharing your best practices, or by changing a government policy or a funding model? By thinking this way, you will be forced to consider making your plans more ambitious and, therefore, making a greater contribution to the world.

ALAN: The Tamarack Institute for Community Engagement started in 2002 to help communities across Canada build effective collaborations across sectors to deal with key issues, as defined by the communities themselves. Its main project, Vibrant Communities, was a wide range of anti-poverty initiatives, working with upwards of thirty Canadian communities. For years the work was intense and very active. A part of Tamarack's plan was always to harvest the knowledge being created by the work: how do we build collaborations, what works, where does funding come from, what are community levers for change? Now, because the plan to harvest knowledge works, Tamarack has a new way of operating, primarily as a distributor of knowledge through training and conferences. It facilitates conversations between activists to keep generating new knowledge that is included in the knowledge transfer. Without the original strategy to harvest knowledge, without an operating plan to record and store it, and without each part of Vibrant Communities and Tamarack implementing the operation plan for each locale, the current robust knowledge exchange would not exist.

Summary

At the end of your planning process, there will be stated expectations for your staff about what they are being asked to do, as well as agreed-upon targets that your board will help you achieve. These plans make up the road map for you, as CEO. They provide clarity for stakeholders and staff, and will provide you with the focus and discipline you need to ensure you are steering the organization to the agreed-upon and desired destination.

TIPS AND RESOURCES ------------------------------

1. James Appleyard's "Strategic Planning" chapter in *Five Good Ideas: Practical Strategies for Non-Profit Success* (Coach House, 2011) provides practical, sound advice on how to most effectively use the strategic planning process.

2. If you think your board might be unclear in its role, consider giving it the article "Planning to Prevail: A Practical Guide to the Board's Role in Strategic Planning and Performance Measurement" by David A.H. Brown and Debra L. Brown (Conference Board of Canada, 2000). It outlines how an integrated approach to strategic planning can set the course for a highly successful organization.

3. "Delivering on the Promise of Nonprofits" by Jeffrey L. Bradach, Thomas J. Tierney, and Nan Stone (*Harvard Business Review*, 2008) highlights the unique challenges faced by non-profit leaders and the ways these challenges can be overcome by confronting questions related to strategy, capital, and talent. (www.hbr.org/2008/12/delivering-on-the-promise-of-nonprofits)

PART TWO:

GETTING THE TEAM

CHAPTER FIVE

BUILDING YOUR SUPPORT NETWORK

As a leader, you need access to sound strategic advice, expertise and skills, opportunities to learn, and, of course, personal support. To a limited extent, you can depend on the existing structures of the organization to provide you with these. Your staff will most certainly have skills and expertise that you can depend on. Your board and committee members will also lend you their support as advisors. These individuals have chosen to be involved because they are committed to the work and have talents that are important for the organization's success.

In hiring you, the board is particularly invested in seeing you succeed. Corporate structures will be of great use to the CEO, but keep in mind that they have an overarching purpose: to protect the interests of the organization. This means that you can't rely on them as personal support systems. Boards have a fiduciary duty to ensure that you are properly managing the affairs of the organization. They need to keep some distance from you so that they can hold

Board Role

you accountable and take necessary steps if they judge the organization is not being well served by you.

In other words, the organizational support structures are not about you as an individual but about you as the CEO. This means that you need to set up your own independent sources of advice and support.

Part A. The Value of Networks

Networks are essential to any leader, and it is your responsibility to develop and nurture them, not only for the sake of the organization's work but also for your own development. Networks spark ideas, lead to partnerships and collaboration, and can accelerate impact. For your own personal networks, there are three key benefits for cultivating a strong network: to have sounding boards for everyday issues and longer-term visioning; to provide you with access to specialized skills and resources; and to provide professional development opportunities.

Leading an organization can be lonely. Unlike the board or staff, the CEO does not have peers within the organization. For first-time CEOs, this can be a difficult adjustment. You no longer have anyone with whom you can discuss everyday challenges, doubts, and frustrations of the job. People will be looking to you for assurance and clarity of direction. When you don't have clarity, it is hard to discuss your thinking without projecting indecision. This does not mean that you can never express doubt; rather, there are many times where it is inappropriate or irrelevant to discuss an issue with the staff or board. It's important to find a group of individuals outside your organization who have the expertise you need and whom you trust to listen to you when you are trying to work through a difficult issue. These individuals, who have been or are CEOs themselves, will understand your role and can be your support system. They can provide you with the opportunity to voice your frustration, give you direct and honest feedback, and help you feel less alone, simply by being there.

A second benefit of building personal networks is that they can provide you with direct access to specific expertise. In addition to the core competencies and skills that are required of most CEOs, such as financial literacy and human resources management, there are other skills particular to leading a specific organization, such as fundraising or political advocacy, and issue-specific content and knowledge that is required to oversee the work of the organization. Although there is always something to learn, a new or first-time CEO may feel insecure or have a steep learning curve in a certain part of the job. Early identification of a group of experts who are willing to provide you with advice and access to resources in one of your weaker areas will accelerate your learning.

The third key reason for establishing a support network is to make sure you don't isolate yourself and your organization from the larger sector in which you are working. Often the immediate needs of the job can result in a CEO being too inwardly focused and insular. You will be responsible for setting the long-term vision of the organization. Sound strategic decisions require that a CEO ensures intellectual inputs; a sophisticated understanding of the environment or market and any foreseeable changes; knowledge of best practices; and awareness of the players. As well, you want to make sure that you are constantly improving your skill set by keeping up to date with best management practices. The most effective leaders are those who are constantly engaged with improving themselves.

> **ALAN:** When Ken Battle and I founded the Caledon Institute of Social Policy, we consulted with a number of people about setting up a success-ful organization, one of whom was my colleague Peter Karoff, the founder and president of the Philanthropic Initiative in Boston. We told him about our conception of Caledon and, amid other information, what our work would be and how we would be funded. He somewhat startled us with his first question: "Who are your peers?" We had been almost completely inwardly focused and had thought little about the context in which we were creating Caledon, the places we might find allies or competitors, safe harbours, or rocky shoals. And as much as anything, Peter was advising us to seek strength in common cause with others.

Seek strength in common cause with others

Part B. Organizing the Networks

Networks, both formal and informal, will help meet different needs, and you will find that having a collection of people whose talents and ideas you can count on will prove invaluable. The actual networks that will work best for you depend on the needs of your organization, your current skills, and the missing experience.

The following are descriptions of a few different types of networks. Before deciding on the structures of and the people to bring into your networks, take time to conduct a self-assessment that identifies what needed knowledge you are missing, what you need to broaden, and what you need to keep up to speed on.

> **FRANCA:** When I accepted the job as CEO, I made this list. In the "need to know" column, I put financial management, legal, and board management. Although I had experience in setting and managing budgets, I had not been financially responsible for an entire organization. The same could be said for board management. I had prepared and presented reports for a board, and I had served on boards, but this was the first time I was reporting to one directly. In my "need to broaden" column, I wrote human resources, fundraising, and communications. These were priorities for the Loran Scholars Foundation, and although I had experience in all three, I knew I would benefit from the assistance and advice of a

> few experts as I planned for some changes. I must admit that I did not even think about the "need to keep up with" column until much later. I was so focused on my immediate needs that I did not understand how equally useful it would be to continue to nurture the relationships and areas of expertise that I already possessed.

1. A Kitchen Cabinet

The term "kitchen cabinet" was coined in 1831 by opponents of US President Andrew Jackson. The term referred to the group of unofficial advisors that President Jackson consulted with during the Eaton affair that led him to purge the official United States Cabinet (the "parlor cabinet"). Ever since, it has come to refer to an informal list of people who are called on to offer perspective and good counsel on strategy, tactics, personal growth, acquisition of critical skill sets, and problem-solving. Some of them may be friends, mentors, or family while others may be relative strangers, but each has something to offer and a willingness to offer it.

Your kitchen cabinet can be set up in a formal, highly structured way with three to five people who meet (potentially over dinner or breakfast) once a month or every couple of months. This type of cabinet works best when everyone around the table has an interest in learning from each other. It requires openness, a willingness to cooperate, and the desire to get along with each other. Ideally, people should have expertise that is different enough to fill each other's gaps and high-level enough to be useful. The drawback with this type of network is that it may be difficult to get a commitment of time from the members, which will make scheduling a challenge. The advantage of this type of network is that you can benefit from hearing the group debate an issue based on a wide range of in-depth experiences. To more experienced CEOs, this type of group may prove invaluable.

Another way of structuring the cabinet is to put together an informal group of people who have agreed to make themselves available to you and who don't ever have to meet. Although the format is informal, you have actually asked and they have accepted to serve in this way. From the outset, you have made them aware of how you perceive their role and what kind of commitment they are making. This step should not be taken for granted as you are asking people to help you become a better leader and to help you with some of your decision-making. You need to be sure that when you need them, they'll take your call and provide you with confidential and sound advice. The benefit of this type of cabinet is that it allows you the opportunity to recruit for specific expertise such as IT, financial, human resources, investment, legal, or marketing, as well as general strategic advice. Unlike the more formal kitchen cabinet or formal organizational structures, such as the board, when you recruit for this type of cabinet, you need not worry about how they get along with others or each other as they need only get along with you. Since they don't meet, size will also be less of a consideration. Just keep in mind that it may take more time to feed them information individually.

Whether you choose the formal or informal structure, you should take the time at the beginning to provide members with information about your organization, and then you must keep them up to date with your work. You should contact the group or each member on a regular basis: three to four times a year just to touch base, even a brief conversation to follow up on the last advice they gave. Keep the contact live and put them on a rotation for calling.

2. A Peer-to-Peer Network

In addition to your kitchen cabinet, a peer-to-peer support group of other CEOs will be of value. Unlike with a kitchen cabinet, you are not necessarily going to request detailed strategic advice from this group, and you are probably not going to be comfortable talking about any serious issues you are facing. Also, you must not discuss any confidential matters, such as an employee's case or details about a board director or donor. However, this group can be extremely useful in helping you think about your day-to-day work and how you organize it, and they can connect you with contractors, ideas, and established networks. You can, for example, contact this group and ask, "Do you know anybody who could help me with this IT problem?" or "How have you dealt with performance reviews?" They can share information about professional development courses or relevant conferences. You will find that you also have skills and resources to share with this group yourself. Unlike the kitchen cabinet, which is there to support you, this group is made up of people who will need you to give them your time, ideas, and expertise as well. You have to commit to making yourself available to your peers and to be willing to share openly with them.

> **ALAN**: Maytree has specialized over the years in various capacity-building programs for non-profit and charitable leaders in leadership, management, public policy, and specific areas like fundraising. After a few years we noticed that some people went from one course to another, and others disappeared. The ones who stayed expressed a desire to keep engaged with us, so we created an alumni association, and we began both to hold special events to bring them together and to invite them to general Maytree events. The benefits have been clear: the alumni help each other with problem-solving on issues like human resource management, information technology, or government relations; they coach one another on career development; and they help each other with career mobility as they advance within organizations or move from one sector to another, say from the immigrant-settlement sector to the arts, or even to the commercial sector.

Of course, before committing to a network with another CEO, you might want to meet informally a few times and make sure you are aligned in terms of your leadership and management style, as well as your values. These relationships require a lot of trust, so don't commit before you feel right — just like in any other relationship in your life!

3. Professional Networks

Your existing professional networks can also provide great value. These can connect you with other leaders in the field and provide you with professional development opportunities. If you are a first-time CEO, then you will have to get used to the idea that, more than ever before, your professional development is your responsibility. You should regularly assess where you need to build or expand your knowledge or skills.

Academic, networking, and charitable organizations offer short-term sessions (for example, two-day courses, lunchtime discussions, evening workshops) on topics such as reading a balance sheet, principles of human resources, or fundraising. This is an opportunity not only to learn but also to connect with people and build networks in those specific fields. Be alert to building up these kinds of contacts, and give them the time and attention they need to grow. You can do so simply by inviting people to an event or meeting over breakfast twice a year to catch up with each other.

Another approach to professional development is to hire an expert to provide you with a tailored curriculum. Formally engaging someone may help you fill in areas that are essential for the job but where you lack confidence. The benefit is that a professional relationship can be custom tailored to get you up to speed or to deepen your knowledge in a specific area. You may, for example, have to supervise a CFO and feel you need additional training in specific accounting areas to properly manage this senior staff member. Hiring someone to design an accelerated program will give you the opportunity to shorten your learning time and provide you with the information you need to fulfill a key responsibility of the job.

You should also join professional associations that are relevant to your work, such as the Institute of Public Administration of Canada or the Association of Fundraising Professionals, and take advantage of the conferences and other professional-development opportunities offered. This will help you keep current in areas relevant to your work and connect with your peers. They may not provide you with any advice specific to your organization, but you will have access to best practices and resources to make the best decisions. As you get more comfortable in your role, you should consider ways to share your knowledge with your peers by offering to provide workshops or write content for the association blog or newsletter.

FRANCA: My first six months as CEO at the Foundation were tough. We were going through a turnaround phase, and my informal kitchen cabinet was instrumental in the transition. I had five key advisors, including Alan, who provided me with essential strategic advice but, perhaps most importantly, kept me from feeling so overwhelmed by the huge task ahead. Having their support fed my own confidence in what needed to get done and kept

> me moving forward through challenging times.
> I also found the two to three peers who were run-
> ning organizations were also essential in giving me
> practical ideas that saved me time and money but
> also allowed me to laugh at some of the day-to-day
> frustrations.

Summary

While you do not need to establish all of the networks right away, you will find that the earlier you can set up your kitchen cabinet, the better. You'll need them most in the first few weeks and months when you don't know the staff or the board. As the new CEO, you did not have a hand in setting up the structure or picking any of your staff and board colleagues, and most likely you will not have many trusted relationships within the organization since these take time to develop. Having your own cabinet is critical. You can take some time to develop the other networks, but be careful not to wait too long. You will be a better CEO when these are in place.

TIPS AND RESOURCES ------------------------------

1. Research executive professional programs that are specifically for non-profit leaders, such as CommunityShift for C-level leaders of charities at the Ivey Business School, or the leadership development programs at the Banff Centre. Some of these will have grants or scholarships you can apply for to subsidize costs. They will help you create your network of peers and enrich your own professional tool kit.

2. Listen to the conversation on social media. Start following people in your sector on Twitter, see who they follow, and build out. This will provide you with a sense of what issues are being discussed and who is talking about them.

3. Think about people outside your professional circles who may be able to provide you with sound advice and feedback. In particular, people who know you well will keep you connected to your personal values.

CHAPTER SIX

MANAGING YOUR BOARD OF DIRECTORS

As a first-time CEO, you are now responsible for recruiting and managing a board of directors. You may have presented to boards or prepared materials for boards, and you may have provided CEOs with strategic advice concerning their boards. Being the key link between the board and the management of the organization is a very different thing. Learning to do this well is a priority. Successful CEOs manage their board to help it serve the organization effectively. Less successful CEOs manage their board to minimize its impact. Failing CEOs allow their board to manage them.

Part A. The Job of the Board

A good organization requires clarity on the board's responsibility compared with management's responsibility. A board has legal obligations and fiduciary responsibility for an organization. This means the board has been entrusted by government to act in the public's interest with the highest standard of care (within the law and ethical standards). Directors must act in good faith and with honesty. In all cases, they must ensure the best interests of the organization are being protected, that any conflicts of interest are avoided, and that personal interests are subordinate to those of the organization.

A board has three crucial roles. It is responsible for approving the strategic direction of the organization; ensuring sound and accountable fiscal management; and hiring and overseeing the right leader for the organization.

Part B. Developing a Strong Governance Model

Good governance is not a one-size-fits-all solution. Once you have been hired as the CEO, you will want to make sure that the organization has a governance model that is appropriate to its size and scope. It is important to articulate this model to your board, staff and stakeholders to ensure buy-in and support. This model includes the structure and size of the board and its committees; roles of the officers, directors, and members; and reporting and decision-making procedures.

A well-governed, healthy organization can have only one type of board: one that will meet its fiduciary responsibilities for oversight and accountability. A board should not be involved in day-to-day work, as it must always have the impartial distance necessary for accountability. Once board members take on operating roles, the lines become blurred.

Who is watching whom should be obvious. Just as staff cannot do the work and oversee it as well, the same is true of board members.

Maintaining a healthy degree of detachment from operations also allows directors the space needed to think of questions and issues that may not occur to someone who is intimately familiar with operations. For example, a board member might ask, "is this project worth doing at all?" — an unlikely question from a staff member who has just spent six months working on the project. At the same time, a board cannot be so detached and irregular in its involvement with management that it does not have the understanding and, by extension, the authority to properly oversee the work of the CEO. The skills and talents of individual board members should always be fully engaged to benefit the mission of the organization, but board members need not ever cross the line into management and compromise the integrity of the decision-making process.

Unfortunately, it is quite common for CEOs of charities to ask someone to serve on the board with the intention of involving them in the operations. For example, you may be tempted to put someone on the board because she volunteered to help you put together your IT plans or is willing to design and manage your website. A CEO of a small organization with limited resources might be so grateful and determined to ensure a continued commitment to the organization that he will nominate the individual to the board. A better strategy is to establish a management committee for

IT and ask the volunteer to chair the committee. You can find a role for anyone who is interested and has skills that will help your organization, but you must ensure that a volunteer is taking on an appropriate role that fits her skills, without ever jeopardizing the integrity of the oversight and accountability that the board provides.

Once you have made sure that your board is clearly separated from the day-to-day operations of your organization, your governance plan should include written mandates for the board that clearly state what is expected of directors. These should include the term limits of the positions, the responsibilities of specific officers, and the formal responsibilities of the directors. The informal responsibilities should also be clear: for example, if a director is expected to donate at a particular level or is expected to attend a certain number of events. You should also share the established calendar of meeting dates and times with forward agendas. Too often meetings are not planned far enough in advance or are rescheduled, which makes it difficult for directors, who are often very busy, to live up to their responsibilities. If they know ahead of time, they can make sure to be present.

Some boards have a document that is periodically circulated to members reminding them of the agreed-upon governance principles. Sometimes board members are even asked to sign the document to acknowledge that they've received and read it. This helps a board feel comfortable with the relationship between CEO and board. Periodically endorsing the agreed-upon principles will make sure the board has the opportunity to tell the CEO what it needs to live up to the agreement.

> **FRANCA**: When I started at the Loran Scholars Foundation, the organization had six committees (finance, fundraising, strategic planning, nomination, audit, academic programming), each with anywhere from four to seven members, and a board of 23 people. We had a staff of six. It was simply unruly. I was spending more time putting together reports and planning for meetings than doing the work. It was also a huge waste of time for the directors. The hours they spent preparing and attending the meetings could definitely have been better used in more tangible and productive ways. We initially cut the number of committees down to two: an executive committee and an audit committee. The executive met once between board meetings and took on many of the tasks of the finance, strategic planning, and nomination committees. The board could manage some of the work directly, and other pieces were management's responsibility. A few years later, as we established an endowment fund and our investments became more complex, we established a separate investment committee.

Another aspect of the governance plan is the size of the board and the structure of its committees. Neither should be cumbersome for the organization. For example, there is no point in an organization with a $500K budget having a huge board with a lot of committees because too many resources will be spent servicing the board.

The appropriate committee structure for an organization should be one that streamlines and focuses the decision-making process of the board. If the board can oversee the work, then there is no need for a committee. In the same vein, if the work relates more to programming, then the committee may not need to exist at all. At times, board committees are established in the early days of an organization when directors tend to be more involved in operations, or they are set up to deal with a specific situation. These committees continue to exist long after they are necessary because no one feels comfortable dismantling them, or because the committees are seen as part of a tradition.

ALAN: Early in the life of Tides Canada, the board was made up of the founding chair and many directors who had served since the beginning. The founding CEO had been working with a board program committee. At one point, it became clear that this early practice needed to stop. Programming was clearly the responsibility of staff, and it was their responsibility to present program ideas to the board, not the other way around.

Once you have developed a strong governance model, you will want to turn your attention to helping your board design a sound recruitment and orientation process for new directors.

Part C. Recruitment and Orientation of New Directors

The task of recruiting directors is a highly strategic one for an organization. A board is critical to an organization's success, and finding the right team of individuals should always be a priority. A good way of thinking about recruiting directors is to consider what windows on the world the organization needs to have now and in the future, and then find the people who have the best view through those windows. You may determine that you need a window on fundraising or one on a specific issue (for example, autism or social finance). Therefore, you will want to recruit people who can serve as the eyes through that window. Short-sightedness is a potential pitfall in this process. Keep in mind that a director will often serve on your board for four to nine years, and sometimes longer. When recruiting directors, you want to have a good idea of where the organization should be in five years (the resources you'll need, the people you will want to attract, etc.). Then think about what kind of team you'll need to get there. In addition, your recruitment strategy should make sure that the board, taken *together*, will bring to the table a variety of skills and resources that you have identified as necessary. This means that you don't want them all to be generalists or to have the same areas of expertise.

> **ALAN**: I remember when I was on a university board, and the chair of the nominating committee came to me and asked me if I knew any good women to nominate. I knew they were interested in achieving better gender diversity, but "good women" was not a helpful category for my thinking. Being aware that a skill the board was lacking was finance, I replied that indeed I knew a great number of good women, but that the better question might be whether I knew any good women bankers.

Another pitfall in the recruitment of board directors is turning a financial investment in the organization into an automatic invitation to the table. It is a practice often seen among venture capitalists who provide funding with the condition that they serve on the board. Some charities use directorships as a perk or means of recognizing major donors: if a donor gives a certain amount, then they are automatically offered a seat. This type of recruitment is simply dysfunctional. Directors should be chosen because they have the expertise and interest to advance the long-term vision of the organization, not only the immediate financial needs. This is not to say that investors or donors shouldn't be directors; many of them will possess the kinds of skills and areas of influence you are looking for. But the seats on the board should not be for sale. This could only come at the price of governance, and once that is for sale, the organization is in trouble.

> **FRANCA:** In my experience, donors do not typically want to serve on boards. Most don't enjoy sitting on committees and attending long meetings. They value their time, often more than their money. A commitment of time should be discussed separately. When someone joins the board, it should be because they have the interest, the skills, and the time to contribute to the future strategic direction of the organization, and not because you automatically assume it may be a good way to steward your donor.

Another recruitment tactic that can be tricky is dealing with representation. It is reasonable that an organization that serves autistic children, for example, has parents of autistic children on its board. After all, parents will have a passion and a sophisticated understanding of the issues. But these individuals should not be parents of clients the organization is currently serving. Clients serving on the board are put in the difficult position of having to separate what is best for the organization and what is best for themselves or their loved ones. At the same time, an organization should always be connected to the people it is serving and include their voices in its work. This can happen by having clients or representatives on advisory committees, on an ad hoc committee asked to look into an issue, or on a program committee managed by staff.

Once individuals are identified as potential recruits, and if they are interested in discussing their involvement, the next step should be a thorough and open conversation. You should provide them with the job description, mandates for the board and the committees, and any informal expectations. For example, if directors are expected to give, help with fundraising, or provide introductions, you need to tell them so. You should let them know how much time you are asking of them, how much reading they will be expected to do, and what dates and times you need them. You should also give them an opportunity to speak to current directors and your chair without you present. You want to make sure you are right for each other. In addition, you should be able to tell potential directors why you are asking them specifically. You should have a clear idea of what you want the person to do, and you should communicate it. By doing all this, you will have clearly defined a successful tenure for a board director, and they will be able to commit to meeting these mutual expectations. Being direct and honest from the beginning is key to an effective, long-term relationship.

> **FRANCA:** Being upfront about expectations of board members is a lesson that I've learned. As a CEO you can feel so appreciative that a specific individual is considering joining your board that you start making concessions, such as not requiring them to

attend all meetings. This usually does not turn out well. Once I started being clearer and upfront about what was required of them, people could give me a confident and definitive answer. In other words, when I started approaching the recruitment process as a mutual relationship, the focus was not on getting them to say yes, but on determining if it was a good fit for both parties. I would rather have a prospective director decline at the outset than manage a senior volunteer who is *not* able or interested in fulfilling their duties. There is nothing to be gained in the latter. Actually, if they have a negative experience, it can be quite detrimental to recruitment efforts later on. I want each volunteer to feel successful, productive, and appreciated for his or her unique contributions.

Once a board director has been recruited, the first six months with the organization are crucial. You should facilitate a thorough and efficient orientation process. The faster the directors are brought up to speed and learn the culture of the organization, the quicker they will be able to contribute effectively. A good way of thinking about it is that as a new recruit, a director is quite eager to serve and do a good job. Providing them with the tools to get to work right away means you can positively channel that energy. You also want to help new directors secure an early win. If you have done your homework before recruiting, you should know how to achieve this. This could mean introducing the organization to new volunteers or potential donors, or providing you with resources or advice on a key decision you are making.

> **ALAN:** I was involved in founding an organization that grew out of another one, which housed a number of skeptics about whether the new organization was desirable or necessary. One of the skeptics, in my view, also had the potential to be a tremendous ally, so I recruited him to the board and asked him to be treasurer. He didn't accept easily, and we needed to have a number of conversations to air his concerns. Once he accepted and began working to set up the finance structure, he became an important architect and key contributor. He stopped being a skeptic, and the other skeptics either converted or faded away. The key to his coming on board successfully was a process of getting him centrally engaged and quickly up to date.

Part D. Keeping the Board Informed

The board's ability to make sound decisions for the organization depends on your commitment to provide them detailed, clear information at the right time. It is worth spending some time to think about your plan for keeping the board informed and what communication tools you plan to use.

It's good for a CEO to keep in mind that, while staff spend 100% of their time thinking about the work, a board chair often spends 5–10%, a committee chair is spending less than 3%, and a board director about 1% of their time. Regular communication and updates matter a great deal. For a board to make sound decisions, CEOs need to keep directors focused and on topic.

A good place to start is to establish consistent reporting structures. All your reports such finance, investment, or management, should be prepared in the same format for each meeting. This will help directors know where they will find specific information. If you have identified your key drivers (as discussed in chapter 3), then your management report should be organized around these drivers. It is a good way to monitor and organize activities. It will also be straightforward for the board to see how you are allocating the resources of the organization. Ideally, the documents for your meetings should be sent in one package at the same time before each meeting. This means that your directors can depend on receiving everything they need in advance, and they don't have to go searching for it at the last minute through various emails or mailings.

In addition, think about providing a systematic periodic update. You could, for example, send them a short e-newsletter or email every six weeks with a summary of the key activities of senior management and the key events of the organization. You could also call your directors on a rotating basis. Find a reason to call them that may involve a two-minute conversation, and see what they say. Let the director drive the length of the call. The two minutes may turn into a much longer chat. If they want to engage, stay on the call. You are essentially checking the pulse.

Between meetings, you should plan for more substantive one-on-one touch points a couple of times a year with each director, and more often for your officers. The time restriction of a board meeting and the group dynamics may inhibit particular directors from providing a more thorough perspective on an issue facing the organization. Working one-on-one provides you an opportunity to get a director's help on a specific issue. You may also want to use these one-on-one meetings to share your initial thoughts on a strategic issue and gauge their reactions. At the very least, it will be a chance to brainstorm on a variety of topics.

FRANCA: Talking to directors individually is particularly important before you introduce a new idea to the board. In my first year as CEO, I made this mistake. I developed an exciting (or at least what I thought was exciting) new idea and presented it at the board meeting. It was the first time most of them had heard about it, and it required the organization to make a major financial commitment. Not surprisingly, they turned it down. I was initially upset but quickly realized that it was my fault. I had not prepared them to make the decision or prepared the organization to adapt. They were right, and I would have figured it out if I had just talked to most of them about it beforehand. In the words of one of my wise directors, a successful non-profit CEO, "never surprise your board!"

Part E. Keeping the Board Engaged

Each director comes to the table with individual strengths and interest in your organization's work. Figuring out what these are and putting them to use will often make the director feel highly appreciated and understood, and will ultimately strengthen your overall work. There are many non-management roles that can provide the directors with a stronger connection to the organization.

FRANCA: Volunteer roles at the Loran Scholars Foundation include being a member of one of our selection committees or being a mentor for a scholar. Each year, a few of our directors are asked to serve in these roles. This exposes them directly to our work, staff, and volunteers. The energy that they derive from engaging with the inspiring and dynamic scholars during this process, I find, makes the overall work more interesting. It fuels their passion for our mission and provides them with an understanding of our work that informs their strategic decision-making.

Board directors can also be successfully engaged by giving them specific roles at the organization's events. For example, a director who is a particularly good public speaker could be asked to make welcoming remarks. Others could be asked to take care of special guests or greet donors. Equip them to serve as ambassadors by providing them with the background on the goals for the event and the guest list, indicating any individuals with whom it may be advantageous to connect.

You may also consider asking board directors to join you at events you are invited to attend, or asking them to go on your behalf if you think they may be interested in the content or in meeting the other people attending.

Events that you are speaking at also provide opportunities to acknowledge their association and contribution to your work. Be sure to confirm in advance that they are comfortable with this type of public acknowledgement. Most people appreciate being recognized publicly, but you may have someone who is turned off by it. The purpose is to make them feel good about their involvement, so take the time to get to know them and do it properly.

You can periodically invite board directors to participate in meetings you are having with volunteers, staff, or donors. Involving them in a meeting with staff can be sensitive as there needs to be separation between management and board, but the board should have opportunities to get to know the staff, especially the senior managers. There may be opportunities to involve directors in a conversation with staff on a certain aspect of your work, especially if a director can provide an expert voice on an issue.

> **FRANCA**: One way we connect the staff and board members is to have a holiday lunch just before our December board meeting. Staff are seated between directors, giving the latter an opportunity to learn more about the day-to-day work of the foundation. It's wonderful for staff as well, as they get to see how much the board believes in the organization and appreciates their work.

Summary

Although the board is ultimately responsible for the organization and for your role as the leader, it is you, as the CEO, who has to work hard at ensuring the board is as impactful as possible. You need this team to have the skill set, the interest, and the courage to do what is right for the organization. If you help the board work at its best, your organization will be on its way to successfully achieving the impact it aspires to have.

TIPS AND RESOURCES ------------------------------

1. To familiarize yourself with the fiduciary respon-
    sibilities your directors have for the organiza-
    tion, read the Canada Business Corporation Act
    (www.laws-lois.justice.gc.ca/eng/acts/C-44)
    or the Canada Not-for-profit Corporations Act
    (www.laws.justice.gc.ca/eng/acts/c-7.75/)   on
    the Government of Canada website.

2. A fantastic tool that can be used as a checklist
    on good governance is *20 questions directors
    of not-for-profit organizations should ask about
    board recruitment, development and assessment*
    (Canadian Institute of Chartered Accountants,
    2010) by Richard Leblanc and Hugh Lindsay.
    (www.cpacanada.ca/en/business-and-ac-
    counting-resources/strategy-risk-and-gov-
    ernance/not-for-profit-governance/
    publications/20-questions-on-recruiting-a-
    not-for-profit-board)

3. Consider enhancing your understanding of
    boards by serving on other non-profit boards.
    There is nothing like being a director yourself
    to understand how to best engage a director.

CHAPTER SEVEN

BUILDING A STRONG STAFF

Good external relations and effective boards aren't enough to sustain an organization. Successful organizations depend on the talent and good work of their staff. Whether the organization has two or two hundred employees, it is your responsibility as the CEO to build a strong, hard-working staff and build a healthy organizational culture rooted in the values of the organization.

The successful CEO creates a management structure that
- is built around an understanding of the key drivers;
- hires the right people, places them in the right jobs, and provides them with the tools and resources they need;
- nurtures a culture that celebrates outstanding work;
- provides opportunities for self-development and ongoing learning;
- promotes talent and terminates the employment of non-performers; and

- provides the internal team with an inspirational presence that does not waver from a commitment to and belief in the importance of the work, in both good times and bad times.

Part A. Taking Inventory and Developing a Proper Staffing Structure

By now you should have identified the key drivers, and you should have a good sense of the business model and the work plan. The business plan will outline the objective(s) that you need to achieve and the key tactics you will employ. This roadmap will then help identify the key competencies, skills, and experiences needed in-house so you can figure out the organizational chart and your human resources needs.

Remembering that a productive team is one that shares guiding principles, you will first want to think through the culture of the place. Is the work culture entrepreneurial, methodical, cautious, or collaborative — or a combination of these? What does the organization value most? Is it innovation, intellectual prowess, fairness and generosity, or independence and competitiveness? This is an exercise best done before you even take on the job of CEO. After all, if the values of the organization are not aligned with your own, then it might not be the organization for you. If, however, the organization needs a change in culture, and you are being brought in to bring about that change, you may have a complicated road ahead. Regardless, you will need a values framework for the organization in order to evaluate current and future employees.

When you conduct an initial assessment of the current staff, start at the management level and work your way through the organization. With the staff you inherit, figure out what they are good at, what motivates them, and what their outcomes have been. You should have a preliminary sense of this from your own job interviews, when you asked the board leadership about the strengths and shortcomings of the staff.

Be advised that the external assessment given to you by people such as directors or donors is not necessarily complete and accurate. Some staff members might be good at endearing themselves to a director but may, in fact, be inefficient. The external input should not override your own judgment. You should have access to personnel files and conduct interviews with your staff that are focused on their past performance. You may even have the benefit of speaking to the former CEO and any current supervisors.

In your interviews with the staff, you should ask a few leading questions that might reveal the high- and under-performers. A few good questions to consider are the following: What resources or support have you received from the team that has made you more successful in your work? What is hindering your progress? and What do you want to see changed?

Once you have taken a preliminary inventory of staff competencies, you can figure out your redundancies, gaps, and mismatches; and you can organize this information into a preliminary management structure. You will figure out what different teams or units are needed, which ones need to grow, which ones need restructuring, and which ones need to be eliminated. You'll also need to look at the team leaders and determine who should be reporting directly to you. In your former job, you may have been used to having a lot more direct reports than what is appropriate for a CEO.

In short, you are drafting a preliminary organizational chart. The structure should not be so elaborate that it obscures the clear lines of accountability. The decision-making responsibilities should be clear.

One major change for the first-time CEO is stepping away from day-to-day operations and focusing on strategic priorities. This includes making the switch from being a manager to managing managers. Mid-level managers are managing direct reports in the management structure and dealing with internal issues. CEOs will instead manage up (board chairs, and committee chairs and members) and out (donors and supporters, strategic and operational partners, and other stakeholders). Stay connected to your management team during this transition so you don't isolate yourself and lose touch with the business of the organization.

ALAN: I can't read organization charts. I grew up with prose and poetry, and with old master paintings. When I see an organization chart, I can understand the boxes with, say, the board at the top and the CEO below, and then the cascade of other staff and their reports. All well to this point. And then suddenly there are dotted lines, and lines that go all the way to the other side and seem to leap over still other lines. At the end of the day, it seems that everyone reports to everyone and has multiple accountabilities and the buck doesn't even slow down, let alone stop somewhere.

The user, receiving a chart by email, can only puzzle it out. Sometimes a great one-page narrative is better. "We have a traditional corporate structure with the board on top, with the CEO beneath, and four department heads reporting to the CEO. But we encourage management conversation across departments, and particularly require that each department head has a close working relationship with the head of the finance department." That tells quite a good story.

Once you have outlined your management structure, you should have clarity on what work can be outsourced. Outsourcing should allow you to benefit from lower costs, increased efficiencies, and access to skills and resources that are outside your organization's key competencies. Outlining the management structure should clarify what you can and cannot outsource. The essential tasks are those directly associated to your key drivers. Those are the tasks that require in-house competencies. The other activities necessary in running the organization can often be outsourced to a business whose key driver is that very task. For example, it is quite reasonable for an organization whose purpose it is to provide a website that gives online support to other organizations to have in-house web-development and IT expertise. For most other organizations, IT or web-development skills may instead be something that should be outsourced.

FRANCA: A few months into my tenure, Alan suggested I think about outsourcing our accounting. I remember thinking what an outrageous idea that seemed. Around the same time, a former board director suggested I speak to a friend of his who was running an accounting business providing services to for-profits and non-profits too small to justify having accounting departments of their own. He put a proposal together, and I realized I could have the services of a professional bookkeeper, supervised by a controller and a senior account manager, for less than the cost of a full-time junior bookkeeper. In addition, because his business provides these employees with the development and career opportunities of the bigger accounting firms, I would be getting top-notch professionals on top of best practices in the field. In the end, it turned out to be one of the best decisions I made in my first year on the job.

In this initial assessment phase, you decide which employees are indispensable, which need to be further engaged and developed, which you need to monitor closely, what skills and knowledge you are missing altogether, and which members of the current team need to leave the organization. This is always a tough thing to do, and one that new CEOs often put off, thinking that they don't want to rock the boat too quickly and want to give people a chance to prove themselves. In fact, too often, new managers come in with heroic notions of their own abilities to improve the performance of an employee who has been a problem for years. They may hear from others, and even see with their own eyes, that a particular staff member isn't doing a very good job. They know they should probably fire them and find someone more appropriate, but they hesitate.

Maybe, they think, *the previous CEO didn't handle them right. Maybe they weren't quite as good as I am. I bet I can save this person and make them a star.* So they embark on this mission. And sometimes they're right. Sometimes a change of leadership works wonders, there is a special synergy, and things pick up. But usually the change is slow in coming, perhaps with hints of progress, but slow. And often the CEO waits far too long, so long that they develop a relationship with the employee making the change even more difficult.

The best timing for making these personnel changes will depend on the organization. It is up to you as CEO to make these calls within the larger framework of the organization's immediate and long-term needs. You may decide that the team is the right one to advance key drivers, or that there are specific reasons for not making a decision too quickly.

> **ALAN**: I was on a board of a Canadian company that merged with one in Europe. When we met with the person responsible for the European operations, I thought he was weak. He was indifferent and ignorant on the key business drivers. I asked the CEO how long he was thinking of keeping him. The CEO replied that although he was aware of this man's limitations, he believed if he fired him too quickly, the rest of the European team would deeply resent it. He eventually let him go after sixteen months. He was right to wait. In that time he was able to establish a higher standard of doing business, build his own strong relationships, and see other high-performing members of the team emerge.

On the other hand, you may instead decide that the organization needs substantive and immediate changes and that, in turn, you will have to make a couple of personnel changes at the management level. You may decide to focus on these alone, and let the managers make the rest of the decisions regarding their teams. This approach is particularly useful in a large, multi-level organization where your management team is substantial in size. The benefit to this strategy is that the leaders are made responsible for creating their teams.

Firing staff is always a disruptive process; this is particularly difficult for smaller organizations in need of extensive

Firing

personnel changes. In the case where a number of people will need to be let go, you may want to consider which parts of the work need to be put on hold until new staff is hired.

Once a person has been let go, there are established checklists, requirements, and protocols. Before you fire anyone, get the proper legal advice, particularly if the employee is part of a collective agreement. Think through the process of terminating someone's employment, prepare the proper documentation, decide on a fair severance package, and minimize any potential legal action against the organization. You will need to decide who else should be told, and when, and have an agreed corporate narrative to share with staff and partners. Throughout, you are keeping your board chair well informed.

When someone is asked to leave an organization, they should do so promptly. This is the same for someone who has resigned. It's tempting to try to keep the person as long as possible, especially if he or she was a good employee, but the reality is that when people resign, they usually check out mentally. There are always exceptions, but they are just that — exceptions. The majority of the time, once someone has been fired or has quit, you should not expect them to take care of the long-term interests of the organization.

The process of drafting a management structure assumes you will have the necessary latitude for making the personnel changes noted above. This is, of course, more complicated when you have contractual agreements with employees that are tough to break or when you are working in a unionized environment.

One of the concerns of letting staff go is the impact that it will have on the morale of the remaining staff, particularly when there are numerous personnel changes being made, or one of the people you are letting go seems to be popular with the staff or has been there a long time. As popular as an employee may be, the reality is that if this person has been doing a poor job, other staff members will have had to compensate for it. Their reaction may well be "what took them so long?" In general, while you can't share the reasons for letting someone go with other staff due to confidentiality and simple decency, you will have to engage other staff to ensure that the functions of the organization are being managed while a replacement is found. It is helpful for people to have clarity on your vision and plans for the organization so they understand how decisions are directly linked to them.

Part B. Selecting the Team

The culture of an organization is as dynamic as its people. Before you hire someone, you need a written and transparent job description that lays out the basic skills required and the scope of the responsibilities of the position. Sometimes employers will do this backwards. They hire a specific person to work with them and then try to figure out the best fit. This is often a mistake because the strengths that the person might bring may actually not be the strengths you need. Before hiring, figure out what you need to further achieve the organization's goals, and hire for the skills and knowledge needed to succeed in the position. While it is tempting to hire for immediate needs, it is important to look at every hiring as an opportunity to meet the long-term vision. Instincts only go so far when it comes to employees. The best indicator of future success and potential for excellence is in past accomplishment. Look at a person's track record, skills, and knowledge, and match these to the long-term needs of the organization.

The actual hiring process should be organized and thorough. You will likely need to interview your top candidates more than once. The interview is not only the opportunity for you to get to know the candidate, but for you to share the values and expectations that the organization has of its staff. You want people to opt out if they know they are not going to be the right fit.

It is amazing how many people hire staff without conducting thorough reference checks. One problem is that employers fear being sued for sharing their evaluations of their past employees. It is, however, essential that before hiring staff, you request to speak to their past supervisors. It is not acceptable to speak to colleagues alone, and you should make sure that the references include people who oversaw this person's work. Their willingness to share this contact information with you may be in itself revealing.

FRANCA: In my twenty years of professional experience, I have managed over sixty-five staff, and I think I have only been called five times for a reference. Amazing! I will never hire someone without

> speaking to his last two supervisors, including any current one. Of course for the latter, I make it a condition of the offer, respecting that people have a right to not disclose this information to their current employer until they have accepted the terms of the position. The one simple but revealing question I always ask a reference is "would you hire this person back?" You either get a very quick and unequivocal *yes*, or they pause, and say something along the lines of, "it would depend on the position."

When hiring, you should remember that bringing new people into an organization is a disruptive process. It takes time to train and transition a new person. You should always have a probationary period of no less than ninety days and use this time to test the person's fit with the job and the culture. Address any concerns promptly, and give people a fair opportunity to put their best foot forward. This usually means that you should have a plan of two to three projects you want them to work on, and you should give them the information and resources they need to start working on them from day one.

> **FRANCA**: Quite often I have seen managers not invest any time in thinking through the first week of a person's employment. You obviously want new employees to take time to familiarize themselves with the organization, and its procedures and policies,

Ⓐ 90 day plan w̄ Sandy.

but you really want to avoid making the first week a passive experience. They need to learn and *do*. You set the tone from day one with regard to culture and values, and having a plan for those first ninety days will do that.

Part C. Managing Your Team for Results

Staff of Code of Conduct

It is good to have a staff manual that lays out the basics of your workplace, such as the code of conduct, expectations around workday hours, procedures for taking holidays and other leaves, description of employee benefits, and possibilities for professional development. Of course, the staff manual is not going to be a motivator for your staff.

Role of CEO

As the CEO, you have a responsibility to provide the leadership that will inspire employees to give the organization the best of their talent. You will set the standard for management and make sure that the people responsible for a job have the resources, the information, and the support to do it. You want to benefit from people's strengths and passions, and to remove barriers to their success. If not, you will most certainly have to deal with underperformance. When you do have an employee who is underperforming, conduct a detailed assessment of the situation. Is the person missing any necessary skills or information? Are her or his strengths and interests well aligned with the job? Does she or he have the knowledge needed but not the drive? If the latter, you

What to do u an underperforming individual

will want to discuss this with him or her and identify possible causes. If you find that the underperformance is a result of their skills being poorly aligned with the job but that they are actually quite dedicated, try placing them somewhere else, where their skills are better suited (if possible).

Often you discover that the root of the underperformance is that no one ever provided them with the training or instructions on how to get the job done, or that they are not using the available tools properly, so what should take an hour is taking an entire day.

ALAN: One of the hardest looking shots in basketball is the reverse layup. This is where the player dribbles the ball down the sideline to the opponents' baseline at the end of the court, then turns along the baseline, goes under the basket, and rises up on the other side, brushing the ball off the backboard and through the hoop. The first time most players try it, they bounce the ball off their foot, jump off the wrong foot, or clang the ball off the underside of the rim. When done by a good player at top speed, it looks pretty difficult.

But when you break down the reverse layup and then build it back up step by step, it actually isn't that hard a shot. You show the players what hand to dribble the ball with as they go down the sideline, where to begin to make the turn along the baseline, what foot to push off with when making that turn,

> when to switch the ball from one hand to the other, where to begin the leap up to make the shot, which foot to push off, and where to aim on the backboard to make the shot go through. If you walk through it a few times, then go a little faster and even faster, often after six or seven repetitions, you'll be able to begin sinking that shot. So break it down, and build it back up. Outline the steps, describe the behaviours, walk through it, and then pick up the pace.

Sometimes it might not be a question of underperformance but of renegade behaviour. In other words, although the person achieves results, the process they use may simply not be acceptable, or may even be in violation of the values of your workplace. If this is the case, first try to address the behaviour without losing the value of their work. If it does not work, it is not advisable to turn a blind eye for the sake of results. You need to keep a high standard of performance but also uphold the values. If people are not meeting the performance standards or are not aligned with your values, let them go.

For people who are meeting and exceeding expectations, you should invest in their long-term commitment to the organization and provide them with continued opportunities to grow and develop. In general, all staff members, with the assistance of their direct supervisors, should create a plan for themselves with regard to their professional development. This plan should address their objectives both on how to grow within the organization and on their long-term career objectives.

In terms of performance reviews, the management literature will outline various approaches from the more traditional annual reviews to the currently popular 360-degree evaluations, where a large number of people are given the opportunity to provide feedback. In general, we would argue that the most efficient way to encourage and inspire your employees is to provide them with regular and timely feedback. If your plans have clear objectives and measures of success outlined, you will know throughout the year what needs improvement, what is exceeding expectation, and what is failing, and you will know who is responsible. Employee performance is as dynamic as the performance of the organization, and you should not wait for formal moments to address it. An ongoing conversation with employees can both encourage and regulate their performance and development.

There is a great deal written about achieving a work–life balance, much of which is aimed at remediating situations where employees work long hours each day, some weekend days, and even holidays, not to mention failing to take all of the allotted annual holidays. Such extended work time can lead to burn out, health issues, and declining performance. Much of the blame is put on employers with a work culture that celebrates and rewards such work habits. Some of the blame is put on employees, themselves, who submit to such demands.

What we've discovered is that people are different in their approaches and appetites for work. Some thrive on heavy hours and total immersion in the job. Others do less well and need to keep to regular and normal hours. Still others work best in a part-time or partial-week role. Your job as their CEO is to be responsive to the difference. Like the coach of an athletic team who knows that some players thrive on being driven hard, be aware of those who do better with regular breaks.

> **ALAN**: When I played sports as a kid, and when I coached sports later, I discovered that some players need a pat on the back and some need a kick in the pants. A good coach knows which kid is which. That sensitivity is important, but it can be overdone too. The coach knows that the objective is to have each player contribute to the success of the team, not merely to cater to individual needs.

Of course you have to balance this with a real assessment of how much valuable work is being produced. Sometimes the "workaholic" spends many hours but doesn't get much done. Or the person who works forty hours a week produces sixty hours' worth of value. Or the part-timer isn't very effective because, perhaps, he misses out on the collegial environment that may be important to his job. Similarly, you might find that some people work well at home while others do not.

How each employee works best?

with employee

It is your job to be aware of how each employee works best and to put them in the position to do his or her job as effectively as possible. While there is no use in trying to force a square peg in a round hole, it is also important to understand whether the square peg is what you need in the first place.

Role of CEO

The role of the CEO in an organization should also be inspirational in good times and bad. You should talk with the employees periodically about the values of the organization. As with any good garden that is constantly growing, it takes constant care and attention to keep the overall look cohesive. Undesirable elements can start to creep in; for example, the language being used by staff to describe the work may become boastful and start hindering relationships with outside partners.

It is good to have a few opportunities in a year for the entire staff to be brought together and to use these times as the CEO to say something about the organization's culture and values that matter and that are worth preserving, such as "we don't have to work particularly long hours but we do have to care about producing high quality work." You want to help your staff members keep their eye on how the organization is doing (formally and informally) in its quest to meet the overall objectives. It's important to call out failing practices without needing to embarrass people, and also to celebrate successes. Your standards should be high.

Staff retreat a couple times a year

ALAN: At Maytree and Avana we use the summer and winter staff lunches as a time to articulate the values of the organization. I express gratitude for the work staff does, our basic dedication to serving the community, our humility in knowing that success can only come by making other people more able to succeed, and our commitment to high quality outcomes. And I always emphasize the value of persevering, of showing up to work every day and working hard, every week, every year, every decade, and taking pride in working in the interest of other people.

Being an inclusive and supportive leader does not mean that you have to take a back seat approach. Sometimes leaders are so democratic in their management style that they always step back and let someone else take the lead. For a first-time CEO, for example, it might feel uncomfortable to take the mantle in front of former colleagues or staff who have been around the organization longer than you. This approach can be as damaging as constantly taking the limelight and making the work about *you*. When the staff is together, they want to see you articulate the values of the organization, believe in their work, and give them the reassurance that you have their backs. They need to see you make decisions and take responsibility for them. Although the decisions you make will not always be perfect, the staff needs to see you move the work along and not wait or waffle too long.

Staff mtgs → productive positive and collaborative.

Staff Meeting

Your main role in staff meetings is to be supportive of your management team. They should set the agenda and rotate the chair role depending on the focus of the meeting. You should take the opportunity at the meetings, as stated previously, to reinforce the culture of the place and remind them of *why* the work matters. Although the atmosphere for these meetings should allow people to be critical of any ideas being proposed, the time should always feel productive, positive, and collaborative. People should feel energized and focused coming out of staff meetings.

Part D. Creating a Culture of Innovation

Once you've set a strategic direction and put together the team, you'll want to work on building a culture of innovation and constant self-improvement. You'll have to set the tone and put processes in place that will encourage staff to be open to critical thinking about the everyday work, with an eye on creative problem-solving and positive changes.

> **FRANCA:** At Loran, we have built in systematic "debrief and improve" cycles into our everyday processes. For example, we ask for feedback from our finalists after interviews, from our scholars after our retreat, and from our applicants and guidance counsellors about any new selection processes. We collect and share the feedback right after any event, and sit together and discuss the ways that we will improve our work. It's an *immediate* feedback

loop that allows us to decide what, if anything, will change. The key is to specifically identify how we will do things differently and what needs to be kept intact. Often changes may look incremental, but we're always surprised how significant they can be, so much so that we wonder out loud how we had not thought about it before.

As the CEO, you want to encourage new ideas but implement a disciplined approach to how they will be evaluated. Change should not be for its own sake.

ALAN: When I was chair of the Canadian Urban Institute in the 1980s, there was enough funding from the city that we were able to pay for everything we did. In the 1990s, the money ran out, and grants weren't renewed. The institute hired a new CEO who came out of the consulting practices with the objective of helping the organization restructure its revenue basis. He often repeated that the organization was now operating within a new environment with very different financial circumstances. His staff knew that if you were going to bring him a new idea, you needed to put it in a framework that would address those realities. That meant you needed to have a budget that would show how the idea would be funded.

How to encourage change / new ideas

The need for the change must be there as well as a realistic approach on how it will be achieved.

Of course, you want to trust your employees to find and implement solutions. You can do so by setting big strategic goals, but then give staff the opportunity to come up with the tactics on how the goals will be achieved. For example, you can set the goal that you need to get 300 people to come hear about a rights-based approach to poverty reduction. Then step back and let staff create and execute the plan. You want to avoid micromanaging. You will mostly have senior managers reporting to you. You must provide them the room they need to take full ownership of their areas. CEOs who rise within the ranks of the same organization should be particularly rigorous in letting go previous responsibilities. It may be difficult to stop doing the job you were doing, but it is necessary. Be careful that you are not undermining the senior manager who has succeeded you in the role.

You may also consider setting one to two meetings annually for an intensive brainstorming session on a specific issue, with the set-out expectation that most of the ideas will not be implemented but that you want people to think outside the box and ideally find a couple of gems.

ALAN: In October of 2015, Evergreen CityWorks conducted a "hackathon" called TrafficJam on the topic of traffic gridlock in the Toronto region. They issued a fairly simple invitation to participate, asking for ideas to make traffic flow more quickly without incurring huge costs or reducing safety. The City of Toronto traffic department made large data sets available for hackers to work with, and hackers were invited to form teams to bring multiple skill sets to bear on the problems. Many were skeptical that non-experts would have much to add to a field fully covered by traffic engineers, but a number of solutions resulted, some app-based, that the City thought could be implemented quickly. The three winners focused on identifying current traffic jams, on predicting them, and on facilitating pedestrian routes that would get people out of their cars. Even the engineers applauded.

Summary

As CEO, you are your team's coach and you cannot take a back seat approach. It is ultimately your responsibility to ensure that you have the right people on the team, that you are nurturing the next generation of talent, that every person understands her contribution and the overall goals, and that you have the best possible support network for your staff to excel and give the organization their best. The objective is for the organization to thrive, and your job is to align everyone toward that end goal.

TIPS AND RESOURCES ------------------------------

1. In her talk, "Five Good Ideas About Managing Your Organization's Human Resources on a Budget," Rahima Mamdani, Vice President, Human Capital, United Way Toronto & York Region, outlines ideas for attracting a strong team and creating the conditions for employees to learn continuously, innovate, and bring their best every day. She also identifies useful resources for managing people. (www.maytree.com/fgi/five-good-ideas-about-improving-your-organizations-hr.html)

2. James Kerr's *Legacy: 15 Lessons in Leadership* (Constable, 2013) is a fantastic read on how to build a high-functioning team by looking at the renowned and highly successful New Zealand All Blacks rugby team.

3. Consider subscribing to business publications like *Rotman Management* or *Harvard Business Review*, both of which share the latest thought leadership on building strong teams.

PART THREE:

GETTING BUSY

CHAPTER EIGHT

RAISING THE MONEY

One of the most important jobs of any CEO of a charity, non-profit, or business is to make sure the money to do the work is in place. This means engaging the right donors, clients, or investors. You likely have experience and are comfortable managing the expense side of the financial statement, but raising the money might seem the most challenging of your new responsibilities, particularly as a first-time CEO.

You may recruit a team to help you achieve the revenue goals, but the responsibility of raising the money is not something that you can fully delegate. You will have to put together short- and long-term plans for how the organization will be funded, be the chief fundraiser in terms of soliciting and stewarding donors, and oversee the key funding relationships. It is simple: the better you manage the revenue side of your profit and loss statement, the more likely the organization will have the resources to meet its objectives.

Part A. Assess Your Finances

To get a handle on what the organization has done so far, where the greatest opportunities for growth are, and where there may be weaknesses or challenges, you will want to spend some time in the early days of your term breaking down the revenue numbers. You should take a look at the last three years of the organization's income to get a clear sense of what percentage comes from which sources. You should understand your donor profile — in other words, who is most likely to fund your cause. You should also study the fundraising successes and failures of the organization and establish a clear sense of how much money you will need to meet your targets over the next few years.

Key questions to ask are the following:

- How diverse are your sources of funding? Are you heavily dependent on one donor, such as government?
- What types of agreements do you have with your current donors? Are you heavily dependent on project funding as opposed to core funding?
- What is your donor renewal rate?
- How much do your events cost, and are they profitable?
- Do you have a sound database to help you manage the work?
- Do you have online capabilities?
- Who are the current fundraisers for the organization?

Part B. Understanding the Different Sources of Revenue

Non-profits have a diversity of potential sources available: government grants, membership fees, revenue-generating practices (such as lotteries or fee for service), special events, sponsorships, and gifts from individuals, corporations, and foundations. The best way to determine what revenue-generating plans you need to put in place is to understand the limitations and opportunities of your organization.

1. Government Funding

Government funding continues to play a significant role in non-profits. The size of public budgets, whether federal, provincial, or municipal, is immense. So it is sensible to begin to explore what government programs might fund your activities. As you do, consider the following precautions:

- Despite their size, public budgets are pretty committed to the existing activities of government. There is not a lot of room for new funding, if any at all. Counting solely on this funding source may be unrealistic. That said, governments do fund some new things, and your organization could be one of them.

- Applying for government funds isn't light work. There are applications to fill out, documentation to provide and assemble, often commitments from your board to solicit, and long waiting periods while your application proceeds through government processes. There may be follow-up requests for more information, which can be encouraging but often don't mean anything in particular. Governments, like most grantmakers, say no far more often than they say yes.

- If you are successful in getting government funding, the third precaution is that governments don't often pay on time. Sometimes they deliberately hold back some funding until the end of a program or funding cycle in order to receive and review an evaluation or final report. Of course you have been incurring costs on a regular basis and paying employees and suppliers. You'll have to find a way to finance the gap in government payments. Sometimes the government is merely late because, well, they're late. They haven't gotten around to making the payment or reviewing your summary report. There isn't anything you can do about this except complain, and that doesn't usually help much.

2. Membership

Membership can be a good source of revenue for some organizations. Where there is a broad base of potential members, and if the organization is in the business of providing goods or services of use or interest, membership can provide a steady and diverse revenue stream. And this revenue stream can be augmented by the provision of special value-added goods or services, such as publications, training, or educational travel.

Where membership is appropriate, the proper pricing of membership is important, as is the proper costing of providing things to members. These are normal business calculations, but they must be bolstered by strong operating disciplines to make sure that costs don't creep up past the price of membership.

You will want to explore whether your organization is suited to a membership approach. Is there a large enough potential member market? Will they require services or goods, or is there a persuasive moral proposition to keep them loyal?

ALAN: Friends of Canadian Broadcasting, a non-profit organization which exists "to defend and enhance the quality and quantity of Canadian programming in the Canadian audio-visual system," has for thirty years been supported financially by tens of thousands of Canadians based on its proposition that it will stand on guard for something they believe in.

When considering membership as a potential source of revenue, consider the following: Can you produce what members want at a cost people are willing to pay? Is what you are going to provide to members central to what you do, or is it an add-on?

Membership is not something you tend to start small and then grow. With a small membership the cost of producing member services is high on a per-member basis. Launching a big membership program requires a significant amount of money so you can create a database system that manages payment, renewal, service records, and other vital information. It may require a website upgrade that will be expensive and time consuming.

Membership works well for some organizations, but you have to be sure that yours is one of them by conducting a rigorous self-examination and a cost-benefit analysis.

3. Social Enterprise

In recent years, social enterprise has come to the fore as a key sustainability option. The idea is that your organization might be able to monetize some of its activities, producing a reliable and predictable revenue stream to fund your work. In the past you may have heard it referred to as "productive enterprise."

ALAN: One of the great examples of social enterprise is the Canadian Organization for Development Through Education, or CODE. CODE was founded over half a century ago, by Roby Kidd and his friends, to ship used and remaindered school books to Africa, a feat they eventually did in great numbers. They subsequently became interested in culturally appropriate curricula for students in Africa and began to fund the development and local production of learning materials. They shipped over duplicating and printing machines as well as paper to produce books and pamphlets on the ground. It then occurred to them, as democracy was dawning in Africa, that printing presses and paper could produce ballots. So CODE Inc. was founded, as a for-profit enterprise, initially to produce printed ballots. Then it became the means for getting ballots to voting locations and back, and eventually it worked on the general logistics for managing elections. The fees they charged for these services went back into CODE's basic work of education, providing a steady source of revenue.

CODE's story is a wonderfully innovative and intelligent evolution that wedded community and commerce. It is an enterprise to admire and to emulate. But it wasn't easy. It took a perfect fit, timing, great leadership, and risk tolerance — and bravery. It made deep sense in terms of the tools at hand and the needs on the ground. And it took some real business discipline.

Social enterprise can be effective for some organizations, but not for all. There has to be a realistic good or service to monetize. You can't wring money out of something for which there isn't a market. Engage in a hard-nosed assessment of the market and whether you have a true competitive advantage. You may think people should buy from you because you have a great and noble mission; why would they not want to choose you over someone else? But they might come up with the perfect reason, for example, that they've been buying from the competitor for years, like them and their product, and don't want to take a risk on you.

> **ALAN:** In the mid-1990s a US social organization decided to open a bakery, engaging people who lived in shelters to make the baked goods. They raised a lot of donations to start the business, and they produced some quality products. Captivated by the social enterprise story, customers came from all over the city. Then two things happened. First, a couple of local bake shops started to flounder because they'd lost customers to the social enterprise. When the old customers discovered this they went back because they'd bought their bread there for years and liked the owners, who were small local business people and, more importantly, neighbours. And second, the people who had come from all over the city stopped coming, the novelty having worn off. It all took less than a year before it evaporated.

To be sustainable, social enterprise must be, in the first place, *enterprise*. The disciplines of creating a business must be observed. It must be properly capitalized; the operating rigour must be put in place and maintained; and the business must be constantly tended and renewed.

If your organization is not prepared to take on the business aspects of a social enterprise, this revenue stream is not for you.

4.   Special Events

For many charitable organizations, fundraising activities are mostly or exclusively focused on running events such as gala dinners, wine tastings, charity runs, or golf tournaments. These events are often organized on the false assumption that it is easier to ask people to buy a ticket than to make a donation. Unfortunately, events can demand huge amounts of time to organize and require the work of many different people.

> **FRANCA**: Whenever people start saying we should come up with a "creative" or "new" way to bring in the money, I know it's someone who is just not comfortable asking someone for money. In my experience, it's more resource intensive to convince people to buy a $200 ticket to an event than donate that same amount of money. Give them the alternative to write you a cheque instead of attending yet another fundraising event, and you'll be surprised how much they'll appreciate doing so. After all, it's the cause that matters, not the party.

Events can be beneficial in providing your organization with benefits beyond revenue, such as an opportunity for public attention to your cause. For example, the CIBC Run for the Cure, in addition to being a successful fundraiser, also generates a lot of media and public attention for breast cancer awareness. As well, the Public Policy Forum (PPF), which has a mandate to improve the quality of government in Canada through dialogue, has used its annual dinner as a means of bringing its membership together to honour distinguished Canadians who have made a difference. While not overtly tied to its mission, the dinner has built the profile of the PPF as a key player in the world of public policy and politics.

Identify the costs and benefits of each event. Start by figuring out the objectives or key goal of the event. Sometimes it isn't as much about generating revenue as it is about community-building, a donor management opportunity, or volunteer recognition. You should understand whether it provides you with strong marketing opportunities or if it generates much needed media buzz.

Once you have a thorough understanding of the objectives, you can engage the involved stakeholders in setting targets for the event. This will require rigorous and honest accounting. Event budgets often do not include the cost of staff time, for example. If the goal of an event is to raise money, set the fundraising goal for the activity, and ask the team involved to provide you with a detailed budget (including all staffing costs) that shows clearly how this is achievable. At the end of the event, the team needs to provide a statement of how much money was raised, net of all the direct and indirect costs (staffing hours, out-of-pocket expenses). If the event is not generating enough net revenue, then ask the team to shift efforts to another activity maximizing the benefits and minimizing the costs. For example, if the spring fair fundraiser with an admission fee is a good community-building event but uses as many resources in staff time as it's netting, it might make sense to simply host an open house with no admission fee, which will not require as many resources.

5. Sponsorship/Partnership

A part of your income may be tied to a specific partnership or sponsorship. This type of relationship differs from other kinds of fundraising in that it does not generate funds to be used for core programming, but it is in itself a joint venture where you and the funding partner are achieving mutual goals. This will commonly take the form of a business giving funds from their marketing dollars to reach out to a certain population, such as McDonald's sponsoring the Olympics, or Tim Hortons sponsoring the Brier. In these cases, the sponsoring company will be interested in who will be reached through the sponsorship, not just the impact the funds will have on your work. This type of sponsorship is therefore well-suited to certain kinds of activities and events, but it will not necessarily be a big source of revenue for small or medium-sized charities that do not have broad market reach. Carefully consider to what extent your organization is able to deliver effectively as a sponsorship partner, and whether it is appropriate for you to do so. We are used to asking potential funders "what can you do for us?" instead of "what can we do for you?"

Sponsorship may also take the form of project-based funding where both parties have shared goals that they hope to achieve together. A strong example is the partnership between 3M and Let's Talk Science, which together created a design competition across Canada aimed at increasing young

Canadians' interest in the sciences, something that matters to both organizations. The advantage with these types of partnerships is that you are getting not only financial support but also knowledge, marketplaces, or volunteers. The disadvantage may be that project-based funding may start to take the organization off course. When entering into an agreement of this type, be sure it passes two tests: mission alignment and cost accounting. First, the initiative should directly advance your overall mission, not be a side project that has little to do with the reason you exist. Second, you have to fully allocate expenses to the project and do honest cost accounting. Overheads should be fully covered, which means allocating hours of existing staff members and a percentage of the rent and other administrative costs. It is not appropriate to say, "Well, we already have to pay those costs anyway, so they should not be included." New initiatives need to make financial sense, just as they have to be aligned with the core values and mission of the organization. You can't do it simply for the money.

6. Gifts and Donations
Most charities engage in some form of fundraising. They bring in donations and grants from corporations, foundations, and individuals and, in exchange, provide the donor with a tax receipt.

FRANCA: Our donors are not only providing us with the money we need to run our organization, they also provide us with the ideas and the people to improve our work. They introduce us to potential selection-committee volunteers and mentors. They participate in our planning committees and other management committees. They introduce our scholars to community leaders and potential employers. They hire our alumni. They ask the questions that force a level of rigour in the evaluation of our own work. Fundraising keeps us in the marketplace, and as such we always need to have a high level of clarity about what we do, why it matters, and how we are doing at any point in time.

The extent to which an organization will have fundraising plans and activities varies greatly depending on the scope of the organization, the willingness and abilities of the leadership, and its history in terms of revenue-generating practice. Indeed, there is not a one-size-fits-all solution, and figuring out the best strategy and approach to fundraising for your organization matters. What will work for the CEO of a large hospital foundation may not work for a small local charity.

Large hospital foundations, for example, are most likely going to have a large team of full-time fundraising professionals engaged in all forms of fundraising, from direct marketing to planned giving programs, from endowment campaigns to monthly giving plans. They are, and should be, targeting everyone: individuals, corporations, foundations, and governments. As a result, they have substantial administrative budgets to achieve their large goals. Smaller charities often have little or no fundraising staff support and are typically dependent on government funding with a few fundraising events.

A first-time CEO should conduct a review of the fundraising strategy and decide where to focus limited resources for fundraising. As you make this decision, keep in mind two important fundraising statistics. The first is that at least 84% of all charitable donations come from individuals.[1] Unfortunately, people who are nervous asking for money usually gravitate toward corporate and foundation grants because they feel they are not asking people for their own money. Even corporate or foundation requests require you to look someone in the eye and ask for their support; and as the statistic tells you, if you are more focused on getting corporate support than focusing on individual donors, you will not just be missing the boat, you may be missing the entire fleet. The second important statistic is the 80/20 rule: 80% of your donations will come from 20% of your donors. If you allocate your resources with these two statistics in mind, you will be well placed to succeed.

---

1   (1) Martin Turcotte. 2015. "Charitable giving by individuals." Spotlight on Canadians: Results from the General Social Survey. Statistics Canada Catalogue no. 89-652-X. p. 4. http://www.statcan.gc.ca/pub/89-652-x/89-652-x2015008-eng.pdf (accessed December 5, 2016). (2) Statistics Canada. Table 380-0076 – Current and Capital Accounts – Corporations, Quarterly (Dollars). CANSIM (database). Last updated November 30, 2016. http://www5.statcan.gc.ca/cansim/a26?lang=eng&id=3800076 (accessed December 5, 2016).

Part C. Hiring Fundraising Staff

Sometimes organizations get into a tizzy when the idea to hire a fundraiser arises. A flurry of thoughts may be strongly held by staff and board members. For example, perhaps they feel a fundraiser should be hired on commission so the organization does not incur any real cost. Investigation will show that this method is rarely successful, not to mention unacceptable in the code of fundraising professionals, at which point your team can move on to consider an addition to staff.

Then comes an inevitable dilemma: the pay scale for good fundraisers is pretty high. In fact, it is usually higher than what anyone else in the organization makes, including the executive director. So the board begins to consider what they would get out of a low-cost fundraising staff member. This will often mean that the person hired may come with some backroom experience in fundraising research or drafting request/grant letters, but has likely never had to do the hardest job, which is to cultivate a donor and ask directly for a gift. If the organization is lucky, someone will shortcut this and ask why a good fundraiser shouldn't make more than the executive director or the CEO.

> **ALAN:** When the University of Toronto got serious about fundraising a few decades ago, it decided to pay their chief fundraiser more than the president. In fact, it was the president who made the decision, knowing that the best fundraiser was paid in a market with a higher pay scale than that of university presidents. In the decade that followed, that university set new standards in Canada for donations and financial support. And this provided a platform for the president to raise the quality of programs across the university, thereby ensuring his success as its leader.

There is a precedent in the commercial world, where sometimes a chief investment officer or chief technology officer will be paid the most in a company. It depends on what drives the business, and it also recognizes that there are different markets for different talents. Having a rigid salary grid prevents an organization from putting the best people in the most important jobs, and from putting its best foot forward.

Part D. The CEO Fundraiser

Whether you hire staff or not, as the CEO you need to embrace the fundraising plan and be a fundraiser yourself. Even if you have a director of development, you are responsible for ensuring that fundraising targets are met.

FRANCA: Raising money has turned into one of my favourite parts of my job. It provides me with opportunities to get to know some of the most generous people in Canada. For the most part, I meet with philanthropists and figure out if their goals align with ours. I never take a "no" from a potential donor as personal rejection. I go into each conversation with the goal of learning about someone and see if there is an alignment. The worst thing that happens is that I have gotten to know a fascinating individual.

Build a team from top to bottom. The board members, as the organization's key volunteers, need to be recruited in terms of their willingness and ability to fully support your revenue generating goals. Of course, not every member needs to be a fundraising powerhouse, but it is a key job of the CEO to think about who needs to be around the board table. If your organization depends on government dollars, for example, having people with good relationships in government departments or political offices will help. Before you ask someone to join your board, you should have a good sense of what relationships they will be able to bring to the organization and their willingness to be involved in that way. Revenue generation is a key board responsibility, and it is easier to raise money if board members have made their own personal donations. But realistically not every board member will be able to donate significantly or be a good fundraiser.

Know the ask. Before asking anyone for money, you need to have a sound plan for how the money will be used. Donors see themselves as investors in the future success of your mission. They are generally not interested in plugging holes, and they usually do not respond to negative pitches, such as "without your $50K, I will need to fire one of my staff." They want to hear how their investment of money will turn into social capital, how your organization will grow and be stronger. You should have ideas specifically based on how that individual's potential donation will help the organization achieve its goals. Before meeting with any potential donor, remember to be well versed in your statistics. In these meetings, the greatest fear people have is that they will be asked something they can't answer, so get comfortable with your numbers: How much money is spent on programs as opposed to administration? How many clients are reached annually? How is the impact of the work measured?

Engage people in your work. Cultivation or stewardship plans should be in place for every one of your prospective and current donors. You should have a sense of where you want to take each one of them and the path you'll take. Usually this means getting donors involved in your work so that they familiarize themselves with the impact of your work. They should understand how their investment would contribute to achieving the goals of the organization. They need to feel, rather than simply know, that what you do matters and is important.

FRANCA: Some of our donors serve as selection committee members, mentors, and summer-internship providers, as well as on the board or on a board committee. I am always careful to first figure out what the best fit is. Some donors I don't involve in any official role as they are simply not a good fit for our established volunteer positions, but I can usually figure out how to use their strengths in some informal ways, such as asking them to meet with one of our alumni who is considering doing graduate studies at their alma mater or working in their field. I have also asked donors to introduce me to potential mentors or organize events for us at their homes.

Do your homework. Chances are you are already connected to many potential donors through your clients, alumni, volunteers, staff, and the people to whom they are in turn connected. Research will help you map these connections and thoroughly prepare you for your prospect meetings. Before you meet with someone, you should have information about their personal and professional backgrounds, their philanthropic interests, and any direct and indirect connections to your work or your people. The more you know, the more likely you will be able to establish a connection. It's no different than a job interview — preparation is key.

Listen, listen, and then listen again. Once you get the meeting, spend most of the time actively listening. You need to leave with a greater understanding of the person in front of you. What are their values? What motivates them to get involved and to give? The more they talk, the greater comfort level they will have with you, and the more knowledge you have on how you can work together. Unfortunately, CEOs in these meetings often fill the time talking about the mission and why it's so important. This is a critical error and a wasted opportunity to learn the motivations this individual might have for giving to your cause. Different donors will give to the same cause for different reasons. If you aren't listening, you may miss crucial information that would turn a rejection into a donation.

FRANCA: Although many of the donors believe in supporting our scholars and providing them with opportunities to fully realize their potential, one of our biggest donors supports us because of the students who *don't* receive the award. For this donor, what matters most is that we are in the high school system across the country motivating thousands of students with the chance of receiving the scholarship to get involved, to work harder, to push themselves. He works at the macro level. If I had not spent the time understanding this donor's motivation, my pitch to him would have been completely off target.

Be specific and clear with your request. Whether it's a letter, a substantive proposal, or a personal ask, the request should be clear and specific. It's not "whatever you can do" but "I need you to give X to allow us to do Y." If you have done your homework, you should know the likely levels of giving for this individual.

Follow up. Before you leave a meeting or end a conversation, spend some time summarizing the follow-up item, including when your next point of contact will be. Of course, call when you say that you are going to call. If you don't get an answer, call back. Most people never call when they say they are going to, and if they do, they don't call back.

ALAN: At least once a month for over thirty years I receive a letter from some organization requesting my interest, engagement, or donation. The letter describes the organization well, makes a good case, and then promises that someone will call me in the coming week. I can count on my fingers — nay, on my thumbs — how many times someone has called. There is almost never any follow-up. I have a protocol with these letters: I keep them in my inbox, either on my desk or electronically, for eight weeks, and then I throw them out. I know what happens on the other end because I have sat on the boards of those organizations. When they are reviewing their fundraising efforts, when someone asks if they've approached Broadbent for a donation, they say, "yes, but he hasn't gotten back to us." They mark it down as an effort well made, and an uninterested donor. I mark it down as someone without the managerial ability to follow through on an initiative, and therefore an organization probably not worth supporting.

Know when it's time to walk away. A funding relationship is a contractual relationship. Mutual benefit and articulated shared objectives are essential in the contract. You should not let the money drive the strategic plan. You have to know where the line is drawn. If you feel they are stringing you along, ask "what can I do to help you make this decision?" If they are still unclear and you have exhausted your options, ask for them to call you when they are ready. Donors are an important part of any non-profit, and having a good relationship with key donors is a big part of your job. But there are risks of getting too close, too sycophantic, and too awed.

Fundraising has risks. The motivations of donors vary greatly. Most are driven by wanting to do good. Some are quite laissez-faire and don't really want a deep operational engagement with your work. Others want to be part of a community. Sometimes their requests may present a risk to your organization. In recent decades the idea of "venture philanthropy" has emerged, borrowed from venture capital with its drama and risk-taking. Venture philanthropy has brought forward donors who want to translate their personal money-making success to your organization by getting involved in the management and governance. Sometimes this can be helpful, if the donor has a rich understanding of the complexity and nuance of the work. Sometimes it can be harmful, if the donor is full of hubris, has a relatively narrow world view, and is impatient. Their intervention can throw the organization off course in a way that can cause you to lose years of progress and relationships. You have a strategy and tactical plans, and you need to stick to them.

Summary

As the CEO, the generation of your organization's revenue is your responsibility. If you can't bring yourself to fundraise or manage government relationships, then don't take the lead in organizations that depend on these ways to raise money. If you prefer the program side of the work, then think twice about jumping into the CEO role, which requires you to keep an eye on both sides of the financial statement.

TIPS AND RESOURCES --------------------------------

1. The Association of Fundraising Professionals hosts workshops and an annual conference that are useful for gaining skills and building networks. It also provides e-workshops and certification as professional development opportunities.

2. Invest in strong research on potential donors/sources of revenue by staffing the fundraising role or finding a solid consultant/volunteer and by accessing fundraising databases that will provide information about corporate and foundation funding opportunities. An example of this is BIG Online database by Metasoft Systems Inc. (www.bigdatabase.ca)

3. In the book *Fundraising Realities Every Board Member Must Face: A 1-hour Crash Course on Raising Major Gifts for Nonprofit Organizations* (Emerson & Church, 2013), David Lansdowne provides a short and effective explanation of "big gifts" fundraising you can give your less experienced board directors.

CHAPTER NINE

MANAGING THE MONEY

The mission may describe an organization's raison d'être, but without well-structured and measured finance, the organization will collapse.

> **ALAN**: People who become CEO of a non-profit organization rarely have a finance background. It happens occasionally, often to good effect. When Robin Cardozo became CEO of Ontario's Trillium Foundation, the biggest grantmaker in Canada, his training as an accountant helped keep order and transparency. Combined with his leadership and management skills, and his grasp of the mission, Trillium prospered.

Most CEOs of non-profits come from the service, policy, or other management streams. They have likely had some budget responsibilities, either on an organizational or departmental basis, and may have had some allocation duties, but seldom have they had charge of the full financial portfolio.

An organization where the CEO is unaware of the status and structure of the finances is one that is open to unnecessary risk. If you are a new CEO without a finance background or significant financial experience, you'd better embrace this area quickly. Even if you don't like it, you need to have a firm grasp of your organization's finances. That doesn't mean you have to actually complete all the tasks associated with finance. You will likely want to hire a qualified finance officer, at least if your organization is large enough.

You can delegate to staff the detail work and the responsibility to manage finance relationships (to bookkeepers, accountants, auditors, investment managers, bankers, and others). And you can trust that your financial staff will develop the right structures and strategies to serve the organization well. But you need enough knowledge and engagement to know if the work is being done and whether it is accurate and useful.

Make sure it serves your mission. The first rule of finance is that it must be in service to your mission. It must be logically structured and impeccably managed, but it cannot be inflexible. No successful organization twists its mission to fit its financial structure. Creating the right financial management regime to help you achieve your mission — in fact, to facilitate your mission — is both possible and necessary. A good question for any management initiative, particularly finance, would be "is it helping us succeed?" The more you know about finance strategies, the more you'll be able to tailor the right approach.

As the CEO, you must have a comprehensive understanding of your finances. It is also vital that your key staff *own* their part of it. Recording and reporting must be done accurately, and they need to operate efficiently. They should take responsibility for making sure the finance strategies employed in their areas are contributing to the success of the mission. They should communicate effectively with you and the finance staff. And they must respect the finance process and the finance staff.

It is useful to have a process that engages staff in the finance regime. Often that process is the preparation of the annual budget, when all of the component parts of the organization prepare estimates of their expected expenditures for the year, as well as any revenues that are part of their work. In some organizations, staff involvement ends when their particular budget submission is prepared, but it may be worthwhile to include all staff in a conversation once the overall budget is complete, taking care to aggregate some items for reasons of confidentiality (individual salary figures, for example). Making the financial health of the organization everyone's responsibility is a good idea, both to avoid unnecessary expenditures and to make each team member an ambassador to potential funders and supporters.

Audited statements and financial reports are different. Your board and the laws under which you operate will require transparency and accountability, and this is achieved through the audit process. Audits produce financial statements that satisfy the law, the accounting profession, and some external observers.

The essential elements of formal financial statements are as follows:

- **The Balance Sheet**, which shows assets and liabilities: Assets are those things you own or control that have value, and can include cash, investments, fixed assets like furniture and equipment, and accounts receivable, which are payments owed to you. Liabilities are things you owe other people, such as any debt you have, accounts payable which are payments you owe others, or grants you may have committed yourself to make in the future from funds you hold now. The difference between your assets and liabilities shows whether your organization is in surplus or deficit. In either case, you need to have a plan about how you are going to either deploy the surplus or make up the deficit. Neither can be left to grow uncontrolled.

- **The Income Statement**, which is a record of money coming in and money going out: The income might be from donations and grants, from interest income on your surplus, or from sales of goods or services. Expenditures will include salary and benefit costs, rent and related costs, professional fees like auditors or consultants, travel, conference costs, and the range of other things you have to pay for. Some income statements are quite detailed while others consolidate categories to make the statements easier to read.

- **The Statement of Cash Flows**, which charts money coming into and out of the organization: These can be summary statements or detailed monthly records. Depending on what kind of organization you are, cash flow statements can be very useful. For example, if you are an organization where revenue appears in lumps during the year, perhaps due to fundraising events you hold or the granting cycle of an arts council, you will have times when you seem flush with cash and other times when it is thin. Similarly, you might have expenditures in lumps. Understanding the timing of cash flows lets you plan better and avoid panic when cash balances are low or negative.

- **The Notes**, which appear at the end of the financial report: The notes are where an auditor will set out the general approach to keeping the financial records (that is, the basic accounting approach, how depreciation of fixed assets are handled, etc.), and comment on any particularity of importance. The notes, which can be illuminating, will also point out any material risk facing the organization, such as if it is overly dependent on one or a few sources of income.

While important for demonstrating transparency and accountability, these statements are rarely useful for running the business of your organization. They lack the specificity. You will know that there are several key drivers to the work you do, and you need to track these in a variety of ways, including the finance dimension. Your audited financial statements will rarely show you that information. For that, you need your own internal financial reports.

Good internal financial reports
- identify and track your key drivers;
- expose how key drivers are financed and presented, usually in a budget;
- track if money is being allocated as budgeted, or is over or under;
- may track cash flow on a detailed basis to enable you to time your expenditures better;
- separate the "nice to know" from the "must know"; and
- help colleagues and board members resist "nice to have" fishing trips by keeping everyone focused on what is most important to your success.

Well-managed organizations understand their costs. They do proper costing of activities and pay particular attention to transaction costs. If, for example, you provide mentoring services, it is important to know how much each engagement costs. Many things are worth doing, but at some point they may become too expensive. Knowing costs allows you to know when that point is being reached and when to adjust your approach.

ALAN: A program that helped find board members for community organizations began as an active intermediary between the candidates and the organizations. When they costed out the activity, they found that this approach was expensive in staff costs and time. In effect, they could only do a limited number of matches, because they were spending too much time on each one. Their choice was either to hire another matchmaker, or to spend less time on each transaction. They chose the latter and relied on the organizations to accept more of the due diligence on each candidate who interested them. The result was a dramatic increase in the number of matches being made, without any drop-off in quality of outcomes.

The audit process is an inevitable part of organizational life but one size doesn't fit all. While audited statements aren't the right tools to run your business, you have to oversee the audit process and make some decisions. The first decision is whether to have an audit done at all.

Sometimes you have no choice: local laws or your own bylaws might require it, or your banker, donors or supporters might request it. Beyond these reasons, you might want it to show potential donors that you take accountability and transparency seriously, and that their money will be in good hands with you.

Sometimes no compelling reason exists, and you will decide you don't need an audit. For example, if your organization is small or mostly engaged with people who know you well, or if you can't afford it, it might be a distraction, taking you away from higher order tasks.

If your organization needs an audit, then you are faced with determining what kind. Do you need a full audit, an audit review, or a "notice to reader"? They differ in degree of information, assurance, and cost.

The least expensive and most rudimentary is the notice to reader. Here the auditor will make sure things are in the right categories or format, and that they are added up correctly. But the auditor won't investigate in-depth or spend time looking for things that don't make sense. And he or she won't provide any assurance about the state of your finances, other than that the columns add up.

The next level is the audit review. Here the auditor will spend more time looking at the business of the organization, asking management to explain some of the obvious issues (for example, staff costs have increased, but donations have decreased; how come?), and looking at a few areas in detail as a sampling of how you manage your records. The comment the auditor will make at the front of the review document, if they give a clean bill of health, will state that they haven't found anything that would make them believe that these statements don't comply with "generally accepted accounting practice" (GAAP). An audit review costs more than a notice to reader but less than an audit.

The top level is a full audit, where the auditor will look at all your material financial activities, talk to management and the board (usually the audit committee), and give an opinion as to whether the statements meet GAAP or not. Material transactions are those large enough, relative to your budget, to matter if they are not done right. Problems with material items present real risk. If you get a "clean opinion," you have passed the audit test. If you get a "qualified opinion," it is not dire, but you will have some explaining to do, perhaps to donors or bankers. Very often these are reasonable explanations, arising out of decisions you and the board have made to serve your mission better. The full audit is the most expensive option.

The cost of an audit is always something to consider. Depending on the complexity of your organization, it can be quite high. If you do a lot of transactions, say by charging fees for conferences or services, produce goods for sale, or participate in collaborations, there will be a lot of invoices and payments for the auditors to review. If it is simpler, it will be cheaper. You might find a sympathetic local auditor who will give you a break, and do it for around $5,000. But you might decide you want to engage a big nationally known firm for greater credibility with donors, and they might charge around $20,000. Sometimes they will offer a lower fee at the start of an engagement, but over the years it may migrate upward to their standard commercial level.

This presents you with a real decision to make, because that $15,000 may make a lot of sense in terms of credibility, but it might be more usefully deployed in the real work of your organization, serving its mission. Recognize you have choices, and determine what is best for your organization. As the leader, you will have to work with the chair of your board and the chair of your audit committee to make the right recommendation to the board.

Summary

As CEO you must own the finance responsibility of your organization. As tempting as it may be, particularly for the non-finance CEO, you cannot ignore it. If a finance strategy or approach you do not understand is recommended to you by staff, or even by your board, it is your responsibility to make the effort to understand it. Failing to do so opens the organization to risk, and opens you to risk as its leader. A finance mishap is one of the most damaging things that can beset an organization. It can unsettle funders, donors, clients, and supporters. You don't want to be caught off guard simply because you didn't make the effort.

TIPS AND RESOURCES -------------------------------

1. Read Warren Buffett's annual letter to shareholders of Berkshire Hathaway. Every year on a Saturday around the end of February or beginning of March, renowned investor Warren Buffett releases his annual letter to Berkshire Hathaway shareholders. These letters are bastions of wisdom for anyone serious about improving their investments, business practices, or leadership.

2. Benjamin Graham's *The Intelligent Investor: The Definitive Book on Value Investing*, (Harper & Brothers, 1949) is a classic that outlines strategies for reaching your financial goals.

3. The *CPA Accounting Handbook* provides you with the background and direction you need to ensure your accounting practices are reflective of current standards. (www.cpacanada.ca/en/business-and-accounting-resources/cpa-canada-handbook-the-standards-and-guidance-collection/cpa-canada-handbook-accounting)

CHAPTER TEN

RAISING AWARENESS

A successful organization needs a narrative that consistently and clearly explains its work and purpose. The CEO is the chief storyteller and is in charge of the message and the way it is shared. Many organizations undermine their causes by focusing so intently on the day-to-day work that they neglect to tell the story of what they do. Crafting and delivering an informative and inspiring narrative that makes people say "I want to be part of that" is critical to organizational success.

Part A. The Purpose of the Narrative

Everybody assumes that if they were better known they would be more successful. In a non-profit organization this is often tied to fundraising. The assumption being that if you are broadly known, appear on TV, or are written up in a newspaper, people will flock to you with money and volunteer time. Your organization's success depends on the ability of your product or service to address a need and your ability to have in place a team of people committed to executing effective strategy and work plans.

A strong narrative is a unifying message, a rally call that helps your staff, volunteers, donors, clients, and potential new friends understand what you do, why, and how you do it. A persuasive narrative draws people into the cause, and provides clarity of your mission. It creates a shared sense of purpose for all your community members.

One of the great failings of the community sector is neglecting to create a strong narrative for our collective work. This must start with the stories of individual organizations, something few are good at telling. We do much good work, often in difficult circumstances — especially those who deal with the hardest problems in the toughest places. And we are so thinly managed and resourced that creating a narrative is always the job we'll get to later, when the real work is done. And often the people good at doing the hard work aren't the ones who are good at talking about it. The problem with not telling our own stories is that we are vulnerable to those who will: the hysterical and sloppy press we're growing too used to; politicians who can ride resentment and distrust to power; or ideologues who want a different world.

A strong narrative explains why your work is of consequence, how it is making lives and communities better. It is mission-based and optimistic, and it describes the problem you are trying to solve without assigning blame for why the problem exists in the first place. Don't be tempted to use it as a way to tell people everything you know. It should differentiate you without getting too complicated. An effective narrative is compelling while still being accessible in everyday language. A person who has just heard it should be able to turn around and tell someone else.

When non-profit leaders don't take the time to tell the story of their organization's work and contribute to this narrative, they run the risk of having it done for them. As a result, the work may be misrepresented, undervalued, or maligned. Your priority is to do good work, but it's also your job to be *seen* to be doing good work. Like anything that is valued, you need to plan for it, budget for it, staff it, and execute it. If it isn't in your budget, it won't get done.

Obviously it's impossible for every group to be well-known. Public attention is not inexhaustible, and you need to have clarity of purpose. What would you hope to achieve with raising awareness? Awareness among whom? Is it important that the general public know your message or just particular people? When do you know if you have achieved your goals? What is the action that you are asking of the recipients of your message? To answer these questions you will need to develop detailed marketing and communications plans based on the needs of your clients and your investors.

Part B. Developing the Marketing Plan

Once you have your narrative figured out, communicate it by breaking it down and developing a marketing plan for the organization. In a for-profit organization, a marketing plan identifies *why* someone would purchase your product or service. In a non-profit organization, this is slightly more layered. Your marketing plan needs to identify *why* anyone would want to fund you, as well as *why* anyone would need your service. You can start to answer these questions by breaking down the sources of revenue and identifying all the different stakeholders of your organization in order to appreciate the motivations of each. That said, be careful of mission drift. You are not altering the message to get to the funding; you are simply tailoring it to find aligned partners.

> **ALAN:** Mark Sarner is a well-respected marketing expert in the non-profit space. He points out that most non-profit leaders, when thinking about reaching potential donors or supporters, will often say "if only they knew what we think," instead of "if only we knew what they think." A marketing plan should help an organization speak to stakeholders in a way that makes sense to them.

There are numerous resources on how to develop successful marketing plans. If this is not one of your areas of expertise, it will be useful for you to take the time to educate yourself. We suggest you start with a stakeholders' analysis and an environmental scan.

a. The Stakeholder Analysis

Review your revenue and expenditures, and list all of your stakeholders: investors (donors, volunteers, and supporters), clients, and their influencers.

In terms of expenditures, you start by looking at your clients or the people your organization is trying to serve, their influencers and general stakeholders. A useful exercise is to map out the life cycle of the client, from their first interaction with your organization to the last moment, in order to understand what information they need from you at which point, and who is influencing their behaviour at different times.

FRANCA: The life cycle of our clients begins with the general population of graduating high school students planning on attending university. At this stage, there are a number of people advising them (parents, teachers, peer groups). It then narrows to the students who submit a completed application, then narrows again to the semifinalists who are chosen for regional interviews, then to the finalists who attend national interviews, and finally to the few who are selected as scholars. The stakeholder group becomes larger with the selection committee members who pick them, and the university administrators and mentors who work with them during their undergraduate years. After four years of participating in our program, the students graduate and become alumni, who may then become board members and donors over the years.

Every organization will have its own life cycle, and you should make sure to take the time to identify yours. As you do so, don't be too conventional in the way you define your stakeholders.

ALAN: In Salt Lake City, in order for a major public transit development to go ahead, the city needed people to agree in a referendum to higher taxes. They had a referendum around each transit line, spelling out what it would cost each person per year. They lost the first time but won each one after that. The reason was that the first marketing campaign focused on users of public transit, whereas the subsequent ones focused on non-transit-using vehicle drivers, showing them how increased efficiencies to the public transit lines would take vehicles off the road and make their driving commute much more efficient.

On the revenue side, your plans will be driven by *who* actually gives you money and *why*. For example, are you funded mostly by government grants or do you depend on private donations? Are you a membership-driven organization or do you sell products or services?

FRANCA: We are a "major gift" fundraising shop, which means that over 80% of our money comes from 20% of our donors. We don't go after government support, but we depend on the tuition waivers of our university partners. Our volunteers are essential as they provide us with the human resources behind our selection process. Our growing market is our alumni. Although young, they are increasing their financial support and are expected to be the main funders of the organization in the long term. Our investors are therefore mostly individual donors/foundations, corporate donors, university partners, volunteers, and alumni.

Reaching new audiences is often considered a priority, but sometimes it is better to cultivate the loyal ones you have.

ALAN: At the Literary Review of Canada, the board was looking at a readership poll showing that the magazine was popular with men age 35–55. Most people were asking "how can we reach out to more women?" One board member looked at the numbers and instead said, "why don't we try to reach more *men* age 35–55," because that's where the market is, the so-called "low-hanging fruit."

Once you have listed your stakeholders, spend some time understanding their motivations and clarifying your marketing objectives for each one. For each stakeholder, you should be able to answer the following:

- What does the stakeholder need from you? For example, do they need information on how to access your service or what the benefits of using it or funding it are?
- What do you need from the stakeholder? For example, do you need them to take a membership, buy a service, volunteer or donate, or use your facilities?
- What are the strengths, weaknesses, opportunities, and threats associated with each stakeholder? (Conduct a SWOT analysis.) For example, do you have strong or weak tools to reach your audience? Do you have access to opportunities that will help you better reach your audience? And what are the potential drawbacks to using them?
- What is the value proposition for each stakeholder? For example, what will a person gain from being a member of your organization or using your service, and how will you be treating them?
- What is the "return on stakeholder awareness" (ROSA)? Or, how will you measure your success in engaging that stakeholder? For example, are you looking to increase your membership by 20%, increase your donor retention by 30%, increase the number of participants, or reach a certain fundraising target?
- What tactics will you use to engage the stakeholder and meet your benchmarks? For example, will you launch a social media campaign, develop a recognition program for your volunteers, discount your fees for renewing members, or advertise online?

b. The Environmental Scan

You need to map out who else does what you do, understand their history, and understand how you differ. In marketing terms, this is positioning and branding your particular offering.

> **FRANCA:** In our case, the environmental scan makes it clear that other scholarship programs are using marks or need as their primary criteria. Often I will start our story by saying, "You know how most scholarship programs out there use marks to determine the long-term potential for a young person? Well, we use character."

Once your environmental scan and stakeholder analysis are complete, you should have a concrete understanding of your marketing platform, or the conditions you are operating within.

> **ALAN:** Invest Toronto is aimed at getting investments into Toronto facilities. They would tell you that they rely heavily on the basic marketing of the region, which is actually not done by them but by the province, through the building of a strong health care system, a successful public school system that provides an educated workforce, and safe neighbourhoods for people to raise their families. Those are the elements for their case for support.

> The job of Invest Toronto is to do the sales part, the marketing platform having already been established by the province.

Part C. Developing the Communications Plan

A communications plan describes the tools you will use to reach your audiences and let them know of the availability and purpose of your service. If you need government to change a policy, for example, you may find that an aggressive public media campaign that embarrasses government will actually be detrimental. If you are running a Red Cross campaign after an environmental disaster, the crowdfunding approach may be appropriate. There is no one answer except to say that relying solely or mostly on traditional media to tell your story is *not* a good idea. Of course, the message or story will have to be tailored to the medium.

> **ALAN**: The emergence of social media is an asset to the non-profit sector. Sites like the *Tyee* and *Huffington Post* are more open to submissions from unusual suspects than the traditional commercial press. At Maytree we often find that when we have a story published on such sites, we get much more feedback and higher readership than an op-ed in the newspaper.

New media requires new approaches. There is an abundance of information out there, and communicating effectively requires an understanding of the environment. A big asset in communications is regularity. Most of us tend to be sporadic, and even when we use the Internet, we stick with old newsletter habits of waiting until we have eight or twelve pages of content. We need to get things out fast and frequently. This means staying up to date with the latest media trends and platforms and, if we want to be really effective, segmenting our audiences accordingly. For example, if you're looking to engage Millennials, it's useful to note that their attention is focused on Instagram, not Facebook. We also need to take a lesson from newspapers and highlight the information that is most pertinent to our cause so that we don't "bury our lead."

FRANCA: I was not naturally drawn to social media. When my peers were getting into Facebook, I refused to sign up. Regardless of my personal opinion, as a CEO, I realized that the organization needed me to fully embrace and use social media to its fullest potential. There is a conversation happening on social media that includes existing and potential stakeholders, and I would not be doing my job if I refused to participate.

Summary

Creating a persuasive and inspiring narrative of the work your organization does, and embedding it in effective marketing and communication plans, is an important stepping stone to success. If you leave the definition of who you are and what you do to someone else, you make yourself vulnerable. Defending yourself against misrepresentation can be costly in time and money, and there is no guarantee of success. Don't make it the job you put off until later — which too often is put off until never.

TIPS AND RESOURCES ------------------------------

1. If you don't have much experience in marketing, *Understanding Marketing: Expert Solutions to Everyday Challenges* (Pocket Mentor, Harvard Business School Press, 2010) is a quick read to get you up to speed with the basics.

2. The communications chapter of *Five Good Ideas: Practical Strategies for Non-Profit Success* (Coach House, 2010) provides an overview of effective communications. Mark Sarner's section on social marketing is particularly useful in demonstrating how to use marketing tools and tactics to advance social goals.

3. To feed your creativity and help you keep up to date with best practices and trends, consider following blogs, such as Beth Kanter's blog on how connected non-profits leverage networks and data for social change (www.bethkanter.org). Follow the LinkedIn accounts of Phillip Haid, CEO of Public Inc., Jacqui d'Eon and Carol Panasiuk who post articles dedicated to helping you communicate strategically to achieve your business or organizational goals.

CHAPTER ELEVEN

RAISING FRIENDS

Successful organizations have a lot of friends, people who may not give money but who will speak well of them in important places. While the whole team (staff, board, volunteers) shares the duty of making friends, the CEO is the key. Good CEOs have systematic ways of raising friends. The temptation is to focus only on the direct clients and investors, and indeed it is necessary and appropriate that you spend most of your time there. At the same time, for your organization to be seen as a leader in your sector, you need to think strategically about who should know your narrative and how you will make that happen, without overindulging and taking your eye off the key drivers of your work. Good friends will serve as good insulation in tough times.

Part A. Who Should Be Your Friend?

Good "friendraising" involves sharing the narrative of your organization and inviting people to celebrate the successes. To identify friends, start by looking at who is in the same environment and whether there is any overlap in your work.

1. People Who Share Your Vision of the World

Charities competing for revenue dollars and market share can, at times, miss the opportunity to collaborate and build their sector together. Rather than competing for the dollars, working collaboratively may actually improve the case for support of your sector, bringing more people to it and ultimately benefiting your cause and your organization.

> **ALAN:** Imagine if you had a shoe store and someone else came and opened another shoe store across the street. Your gut reaction would probably be negative, and you'd start to figure out how you would compete and drive them out of business. You may instead seize the opportunity and think about how to turn your street into *the* place where everyone comes to buy shoes. Your efforts may be better placed in convincing more people to open up shoe stores than in competing. Rather than scrabbling for market share, you might try to increase the size of the market.

Regardless of the sector (health, education, social justice, environment, the arts), there are advantages to getting to a co-operative rather than competitive position on the importance of each other's endeavours. Co-operation is more likely to draw people into your work. At the very least, you need to decide how you will share the space, and at what point it will be necessary to work together to be more effective.

ALAN: In the US, a number of right-wing advocacy groups in Washington that had been quite critical of each other started to realize that their public disagreements were resulting in left-wing groups getting a lot more wins. As a result, they came together and created a loose organization where every Tuesday morning the heads of the right-wing groups would get together. The only excuse for not being at the Tuesday breakfast meeting was that you had a meeting with the President or Vice President. Outside of that, you had to attend, and you had to commit to stopping your public criticism of others in the group. In fact, you had to be seen to be on their side. If you breached these rules, the other groups would conspire to get you fired. They realized that they were spending their time on the 10% of issues they disagreed on, as opposed to the 90% on which they agreed. By not letting the 10% divide them, they all became a lot more effective.

2. People Who Have Influence in Your Sector

Identify key decision-makers and leaders in your sector who will be able to advance your work. Spend some time identifying who should be aware of and think well of the work of your organization. Be careful not to waste too much time and too many resources here. You want to determine who within the public and private sectors should know your work (beyond your investors and potential investors). Is it the bureaucracy or the political leadership that should be aware of your work? Which department and what position? Is it the CEO of a company or someone else within the business that you should target? Be highly structured in your approach to this exercise or you may risk squandering your limited resources.

> FRANCA: We want the Loran Scholar brand to be recognized and supported by those in hiring positions, so we have identified human resource executives as good potential friends. It will be useful to them and to our alumni if they know how to distinguish the Loran Award from other undergraduate and graduate scholarships.

3. People Who Know Your People

Some individuals are great networkers. They are present in your circle of influencers and supporters. It is important that they know about your work because they are connectors: donor advisors or estate planners; social media personalities with a significant following; respected leaders in the sector whose positive opinions matter; or other successful leaders and fundraisers in other sectors.

> FRANCA: I often find myself talking about other causes and other great organizations with my donors. If I know someone is doing great work in a field the

donor or volunteer is interested in, I love connecting them. There is a terrific organization called Outside Looking In, which is trying to address the high dropout rate on reserve high schools by using dance. I'll talk about it with anyone who could help. They might be dealing with a completely different issue than our organization, but essentially we both believe in providing young people with the opportunities to reach the fullest expression of their potential. Why wouldn't I want to support that?

4. People Who Are No Longer Involved

Whether they are old friends or former influencers, you want to keep a few good old friends in the know about your work. They may no longer be deeply invested, but as former investors or friends, they may continue to be supportive. You don't want them to say, "I used to be involved with them, but I have no idea what they are up to anymore."

Before you reach out to anyone, you should, of course, do your homework, and make sure that there aren't any fundamental disagreements in your approach that might result in your inadvertently offending someone. For example, you should know if your organization or your partners have said something publicly in the past that could be taken as a criticism of that organization or individual's work.

> **FRANCA**: One thing we do is to host an annual or bi-annual lunch or dinner with the past chairs of the foundation. It is a great way for your current board leadership to benefit from the experiences of your past, but it also keeps your past champions involved and supportive.

Part B. How to Make Friends and Keep Them

You will need to be disciplined and structured in your approach to making friends. Since the gains are usually not as obvious as they are with your fundraising prospect list, it's easy to forget about doing this. Fortunately, there are some simple ways to go about it.

a. **One-On-One Meetings**

Make a set number of calls, scheduling monthly meetings or meals with key people. To be strategic, you may want to create a list quarterly or semi-annually to guide this work. For some, one meeting may be sufficient while others may require a couple of visits per year.

Listen to the specific needs of each individual and tailor scheduling with their needs and expectations in mind. If you have been referred to someone, follow up assiduously. Nothing looks worse than failing to follow up. They'll think you can't get the job done, so why would they want to associate with you?

b. Informal and Formal Friendraising Events

You might consider hosting events aimed at friend-making or friend-keeping. Again, be strategic and set targets around the number of meetings and guest lists. Also, remember that it is a main role of your board directors to make friends. Key volunteers or board directors could host these informal gatherings in their homes.

ALAN: Some organizations host more public friend-raising events. The Literary Review of Canada (LRC), for example, hosts a speakers' series that invites leading thinkers to introduce provocative ideas and solutions on key issues. Much of the audience consists of LRC subscribers, while approximately 60% of attendees are members of the public attending for the first time. They are provided with an opportunity to connect with each other and network before and after the speaker delivers a forty-five-minute talk. Similarly, at Maytree we host a lunch and learn series called Five Good Ideas, where industry experts discuss practical ideas on key management issues facing non-profit organizations. After the speaker delivers his or her talk in five concise points, the audience, which consists primarily of practitioners in the non-profit sector (board members, volunteers, managers, and executive directors), has the opportunity to discuss the ideas presented. Very often, new connections are formed, and in the session evaluations most participants indicate that in addition to professional development, they attend the series for the opportunity to connect with like-minded people.

FRANCA: To engage the senior academic leadership of our universities we host annual receptions at our university campuses with current and past Loran scholars of the university. These events provide an opportunity for us to acknowledge and reinforce our partnership, speak publicly about our shared values, and give new university faculty/administrators an opportunity to better understand our work.

c. **E-Newsletter Lists**

An e-newsletter is an easy and cost-effective way of keeping friends — new and old — in the loop. The very act of receiving it keeps you relevant in their minds. Be organized enough that all the people you meet end up on your e-newsletter list (as appropriate and within privacy guidelines, of course). Communicate frequently enough that they remember who you are and strategically enough that they care about what you do. Including news from other organizations provides an opportunity to build relationships by supporting their work.

d. Emeritus Advisory Councils

You might want to put your old friends on advisory councils or recognize them with an emeritus title. This is great for people who are happy to continue being your friend, and are content enough to periodically help you, but are reluctant to commit time or take a job. Formalizing their role may provide you an opportunity to get the most out of them. Tell them you will meet them once or twice a year, and then make sure to do it.

ALAN: The Toronto Public Library, the world's busiest public library system, developed a Governor's Council to help attract support. The Council doesn't meet as a complete group, but members are invited to all major library functions. Individual members are invited to participate in appropriate funding calls, or are asked to help garner political support when the library is under threat. The Toronto Public Library is very wise in its use of the Governor's Council members, neither overtaxing them nor leaving them unused.

e. Attending Relevant Events

Attend research conferences related to your work and seek out speaking opportunities where you can deliver a relevant message. Tailor your narrative for the group.

> **ALAN**: The Community Benefit Agreement (CBA) model has been adopted in many countries, including the United States, United Kingdom, and now Canada, to connect local community members with jobs on publicly funded infrastructure projects. To build support, an anti-poverty group may speak to a construction convention about the benefits of CBAs.

f.   Old-Fashioned Notes

Making friends is also quite organic. If you read in the paper of someone's good work, send her a note about it and congratulate her. If you meet someone at a conference, have the discipline to follow up with a note, either handwritten or electronic, and ask for a meeting. Pass on compliments you've heard about that person or his work.

> **FRANCA**: After I meet with someone, I debrief and write down pertinent information that I do not want to forget — from their kids' impending weddings and graduations, to their interests and hobbies and favourite authors. I love to send someone an article or a book I know they'll love, or a note before a major event in their lives.

Summary

Friendraising is as much about knowing whom you should be friends with as it is knowing how to make and keep the friends you have. Investing the time to cultivate these relationships will be beneficial to both you and your organization. Don't get so caught up as the CEO in the immediate needs and relationships of the organization that you forget to invest in these relationships.

TIPS AND RESOURCES -----------------------------

1. Invest in relationship management databases. Take the time to research which is the right platform for the specific needs of your organization, keeping in mind that you will need to keep track of basic information such as when you've contacted people; notes from those meetings; how they engage in your work; what and when the next point of contact needs to be; and who else in your community they are connected to and in what capacity. You may consider soliciting advice from resources such as "A Few Good Tools: Low-Cost Constituent Databases" (TechSoup Canada, 2007). (www.techsoupcanada.ca/learning_centre/articles/a_few_good_tools_low_cost_constituent_database)

2. The memoir *Thumper: The Memoirs of the Honourable Donald S. Macdonald*, (McGill-Queen's University Press, 2014) by Donald S. Macdonald, a former Cabinet minister under Prime Minister Trudeau, contains some compelling friendraising anecdotes. It begins, "[at] a certain point in our lives we are left only with our close relationships and our clear recollections."

3. In the book *Forces for Good: The Six Practices of High-Impact Nonprofits* by Leslie R. Crutchfield and Heather McLeod Grant (Jossey-Bass, 2008), chapter 5: "Nurture Nonprofit Networks" offers useful tips on how collaborating with other organizations can lead to more impactful movements and organizations.

PART FOUR:

GETTING ON

J

CHAPTER TWELVE

KNOWING WHEN IT'S TIME TO GO

It can be difficult to figure out the right time for a leader to move on. Unlike any other job you have held, leaving the first organization you've led can be particularly difficult and emotional. This can be especially true for founders. Everyone will have an opinion to share with you on this issue, and these ideas will conflict. "Leaders should stay no less than five and no more than eight years." "If you stay too long, people are not going to see you as the leader of any other organization." "If you are not happy anymore, you should leave." "What are you going to do next?" (Subtext: isn't it time for you to leave?) You will hear these statements and variations of them. Board directors or donors might start to say, "I'll join the board, but you have to tell me you won't leave during my term." You might get pressure from people who want your job. Deciphering your own feelings about your ability and interest in continuing to lead your organization can at times be difficult.

Your timing in making the decision can be everything. Whether you should stay or go will depend on the organization's health, the stage of its development, and your own career aspirations or personal circumstances. Although making sure the organization is able to benefit from the right leader at the right time can require you to make room for the next CEO, you should try to decipher the various signs that might point that way.

Understanding the Signs

There will always be moments during your tenure that make you question "is it time for me to go?" Different conditions may raise the question.

The organization hits rough times. Being the CEO means that when the tough times come, and they always do, the responsibilities will be stressful. After a few of these, you may feel the need to quit. Regardless, it is your job to lead until the very last moment of your tenure.

> **FRANCA:** I've definitely gone through a few highly stressful periods. The job is lonely and the risk of personal failure can feel high, so when you are facing big challenges — personal or professional, it is natural to want to preserve yourself by fleeing. My mantra in these moments is the same one I've used on challenging hikes when I'm either at the end of my rope or going through a tough patch: just look to your boots and put one foot in front of the other.

> Eventually, you will get through it, and the more often this happens to you as a leader, the more confidence you build in knowing that you don't need to flee, but you can stay and see things through.

You are tired. The responsibility of running an organization can be an exhausting weight to carry. This is exacerbated when leaders feel that a holiday is a luxury they cannot afford to take. Unfortunately, this attitude will cost the organization dearly as you can run yourself down and resign before you should. Everyone needs time to recharge and get inspired. In other words, it is your responsibility as a leader to take time away from the everyday, feed your creativity, and get perspective. You don't need to quit to take a holiday or a break. The decision to quit should not be made when tired. You should ideally be in a positive frame of mind.

You run into major conflicts with your board or staff. There will be times when a CEO and member(s) of the board disagree, or when a staff member makes things difficult. You might have to manage something unpleasant. Or it might be more serious, where a board or market forces change so substantively that you are no longer interested in being there.

A board can change dramatically if, for example, a new large donor asks for several board seats and then actively tries to change the focus of the organization. Or technology can change an organization's business, such as eliminating a print publication program in favour of an online communication strategy. In either case, the changes may take the organization in a direction that the current CEO doesn't like or doesn't have the skill set to succeed in.

You are bored. An organization will run in cycles, and after a few times around, the idea of having to do the same thing one more time might be too much to bear. It could be that you are a turnaround type of leader. You like turning chaos into order, and once the organization gets to the more stable stage, you are bored. In general, you have to figure out if it's just a period that you have to work through or you need another or bigger challenge.

> **FRANCA:** At the foundation, I've gone through three huge periods of development, and am now in the fourth. I started in the turnaround phase, where I felt I was fighting fires daily, fixing huge problems, and launching new initiatives. Then we moved to a stabilization phase where process and procedures were documented and followed, and then to a restructuring phase where our financial model required a major overhaul. We are currently starting our growth phase. These phases and challenges have kept me deeply engaged as I've seen huge professional and personal growth potential in each one.

You get headhunted. You may not have contemplated leaving, but a great opportunity comes your way that you feel you can't refuse. Sometimes you may be so flattered when the headhunter calls that you start thinking you should take the other job. Be careful with this one. "The grass is greener on the other side" syndrome may be at play here. Remember that it is a headhunter's job to provide a roster of qualified candidates. It's not necessarily that someone else appreciates you more. Most organizations are bad at telling you how highly you are valued, so when someone comes and gives you that affirmation, you might be seduced.

Succession pressures from below. You have been in the job a few years now, and there may be a member of your senior team who feels ready to step up. You fear that if you don't make room, you may risk losing this person from the organization.

It is rare for CEOs to come suddenly to the realization that they want to leave. Often there is a long period of ambiguity: on the one hand, a desire for new challenges; on the other, a sense of goals still to accomplish and staff to be nurtured. This ambiguity can be settled sometime if there is an obvious and talented successor who can continue the progress toward the goals, and who has good relationships with the staff.

There is a drop in support for your work or the rise of a competitive organization. The role of the organization is not as relevant or as timely as it used to be. You might have been working toward a substantive policy change and once it is implemented, you don't see any reason to stay. There may be the increasing success of another organization with an equal mandate that is making your own work less relevant. If the latter, you might want to discuss with your board the potential of merging the organizations. In general, you'll feel that the landscape has changed substantially and that your leadership is no longer needed in the same way.

You stop believing you can be the effective leader of the organization. It may be that you have outgrown the organization. You don't see how it will grow further under your leadership. This will be a good time to go through the chart of what you are good at, what you like to do, what you are not good at, and what you don't like to do, as discussed in the first chapter. Does your current chart still align with your job? Or is it showing you that there isn't a fit any longer?

In these moments of doubt, take the time to figure out whether you need to prepare to go, or address the immediate issues that are making you feel like you should. Be careful in your choice of confidants. Even if you have a terrific board chair, it is not appropriate to discuss a potential departure with your chair until you are seriously considering it. The same goes for the stakeholders of the organization. It would be difficult for them to trust that you are still committed to the organization if you decide to stay after you've discussed your doubts about staying. You may want to keep your discussions to your personal support network, as discussed in chapter five.

Summary

If you are certain that it is time to go, remember that leaving is not a lack of loyalty. There is a benefit to society when you keep challenging yourself, and a benefit to the organization that can continue to grow under someone else's leadership. Above all, don't fall into the trap of thinking your organization won't find a leader as good or as committed as you. If you've done your job well, the organization will attract outstanding candidates eager to take the lead.

TIPS AND RESOURCES ------------------------------

1. The organizational life cycle model is a well-established management process that identifies five stages: start-up, growth, maturity, productivity, and ending. It can be used for teams and organizations but also for individuals as a way to help you gauge what stage you're in and what is required for you to move to the next one. In moments of transition, it is a good model to revisit. You can use it to identify what the stage requires of you as a leader.

2. In his book *Why Nonprofits Fail* (Jossey-Bass, 2004), Stephen R. Block outlines how organizations can be stymied by inflexible leaders with the best intentions. Chapter 11: Founder's Syndrome is particularly useful in addressing

some of the specific issues associated with founders and the difficulty they face in letting go.

3. In the online publication *The CEO Life Cycle* (Wiley, 2015), author Manfred F. R. Kets de Vries outlines three stages of being a CEO: entry, consolidation, and decline. He suggests that the major challenge for many CEOs is recognizing when the moment has come to move on. (www.onlinelibrary.wiley.com/book/10.1002/9781119206477)

CHAPTER THIRTEEN

PREPARING FOR THE NEXT LEADER

Great CEOs leave organizations better than they found them, poised to embrace the future. How do they do it? They build leaders in their staff so that their departure does not leave a void, and so that the board will have some internal candidates to consider for succession. They also build leaders in key volunteers and bring friends into the organization who could be potential candidates.

This is not an activity for the last six months, but one that starts on your first day. A culture of writing things down and documenting relationships, business processes, and policies will help the next leader succeed. It is important to leave strong programs and a strong business plan that is realistic and flexible. This, along with strong internal leaders and a resilient and flexible culture, sets an organization up for continued success.

Although it is ultimately the board's responsibility to hire the CEO, remember that until your successor is appointed, it is up to you to ensure the organization succeeds.

Part A. Giving Your Notice

How much advance notice you give your board might depend on the reason you are leaving. You don't want to leave your organization in the lurch with very short notice of only a few weeks. At the same time, you don't want to burden it with a very long notice, during which time you become a lame duck. Some CEOs give a year's notice or more, which is far too long. On the one hand, staff, board, and stakeholders quickly begin to look beyond the current CEO, sapping their influence and power. And on the other hand, the CEO begins to check out, sapping their own effectiveness. Once someone makes the decision to leave, they begin to check out subconsciously. Generally, a notice period for a CEO is between six and twelve weeks, but this will depend on your organization.

> **ALAN:** After a number of years in my first leadership job, I decided I wanted to move on, which I knew would be a surprise to my board, all of whom were CEOs in their own companies. I thought I was being fair to them by giving them six months' notice, and they seemed to think so too. But immediately their thoughts turned to succession, and after six weeks they were beginning to tune me out. They identified my successor after a couple of months, and an awkward four months of overlap ensued, with my successor encouraging me to take a lot of time off in the last couple of months. In retrospect, six to eight weeks' notice would have been plenty.

Your board chair should be the first person to learn of your decision, and together you should decide on a communication plan and timeline to announce your departure.

Part B. Guiding the Process, Not the Decision

You should not be involved in choosing your successor, but you can help the board prepare a search process, including deciding when and how to make it public. A good board will appreciate this initial help but likely not want you to be involved further. This is appropriate and should not be taken personally.

The following outlines the steps that may be taken to guide a smooth transition:

1. The board may start by assigning a key director (often the chair) to oversee the process and determine the membership of the selection committee.

2. The board should decide early in the process on whether a search firm should be hired to do the intake and first screening of the applicants. You may want to help them generate a list of firms with strong links in your specific industry. If they are not going to use a firm, they need to determine the process they will use to find the candidates.

3. You should give the key directors (or search committee members) a list of donors and key stakeholders who will need to be consulted. As a starting point, they might consider calling key stakeholders to ask: "What do you think are the key challenges and

opportunities for the organization in the next five to ten years? What qualities should the CEO bring to the organization? Is there anyone we should be considering?"

4. You should provide them with a letter with the following: your opinion on the strategic challenges and opportunities for the organization; a list of industry leaders and potential channels to find candidates; any names of individuals you believe should be included in the search; information on the current management team that is relevant; and your opinion on the next model for leadership. The latter is particularly important as a board can get caught in thinking that the success or failure of their current leader means the need to find either a CEO who is either the same as or opposite to you. The same organization at different stages will need different types of leaders.

5. You should provide them with a draft job description and posting, which they may finalize once they complete their consultation process.

6. You might advise them on the distribution channels for the posting.

7. Then stay out of the way. It is not your job to find the next CEO. After the process is in place, your focus is to make sure you prepare a comprehensive document to hand over to your successor.

Part C. The Last Few Months

Once you've helped put the board process in place, you should continue to lead the organization until your departure date. The organization will and should change under a new CEO. Although tempting, don't make long-term commitments or other binding arrangements during this process without the explicit agreement of the board or board chair.

Equally important, create an exit plan that will properly allow you to transition the key organizational relationships to the next leader or to the chair. At the same time, it should be business as usual until the very end. The transition period must also be brief. The staff and stakeholders shouldn't get caught in a long goodbye. And don't allow your own personal anxieties about leaving to filter through to your staff.

Once you've left, make a clean break. You should not be exerting influence over your successor. This may seem obvious, but it is amazing how often a departed CEO either meddles in his or her old organization, or allows him- or herself to be drawn back into its affairs by a staff or board member. It is always a bad idea.

Many CEOs think of legacy in personal terms, how they want people to think about them. Successful CEOs think of it in organizational terms. From day one, these CEOs have asked the question, "What will success look like?" and set goals in that context. If you have built an organization that responds to the needs of your stakeholders, your legacy will take care of itself. The ultimate legacy is an organization that continues to thrive and grow long after you're gone. Creating a document to establish your legacy might work in politics, but it seldom works in real life.

Part D. The End Is the Beginning

Whether you already have your next job lined up or are taking some time off, during the transition, you should take a thorough look back and take stock of what you've learned in this role about yourself as a leader.

> **FRANCA:** For me, this book is my thorough look back on my journey to becoming and being a CEO. It has made me aware of my growth as a CEO. It has matured my thinking about my role in guiding an organization toward good governance and good management. It has also given me confidence in the skills I've gained and helped me become more self-aware as a leader.

Ideally, if you've been taking care of your own professional development, you've been preparing yourself for the next step. Before you jump to your next challenge, take the time to properly give closure to the current chapter. Being the CEO has meant carrying the massive responsibility for the organization. Plan that first day or week that you will wake up without it, and be prepared to feel a sense of loss.

Summary

Depending on the length of time you've been with an organization, or how deeply you've been aligned with its mission, you may need to take some time off before jumping into your next CEO role. But our hope is that you jump in again. We need good leaders who are willing to advance the missions of organizations with integrity, commitment to excellence, and true passion for the work. We need you to be *it*(!) again, and again, and again.

TIPS AND RESOURCES --------------------------------

1. The best legacy you can leave is for the organization you've led to continue to thrive after you leave. That's the key message in the article "The CEO's Real Legacy" (*Harvard Business Review* 82.11, 2004, pp. 51–58) by Kenneth W. Freeman. (www.hbr.org/2004/11/the-ceos-real-legacy)

2. As part of the governance-based series *20 Questions Directors Should Ask* by the Canadian Institute of Chartered Accountants, there is a section "About CEO Succession" by Peter Stephenson and Guy Beaudin. It is a useful resource for your board directors to help them identify the key issues in putting together a strong succession plan.

3. The TED Talk by architect William McDonough on his book *Cradle to Cradle* provides a great reminder of how every end is a new beginning.

ACKNOWLEDGEMENTS

ALAN BROADBENT: *You're It!* would not have been written without Franca Gucciardi's determination, perseverance, and hard work. These are the very qualities, of course, which have made her such a successful CEO at Loran, and such a pleasure to learn and grow with over the years. Franca made sure we sat across from each other at my partner's desk regularly, despite our busy schedules, and engaged on the topic of each chapter. Abetting her along the way was my colleague Vali Bennett, who somehow manages to point me in the right direction and make sure I show up.

Thanks also goes to our team at Avana Capital and Maytree who helped organize the elements of the book. Markus Stadelmann-Elder used his great communication and production skills to pull the project together, and Sarah Gledhill brought her considerable design skills to the task. Tina Edan reviewed early outlines and drafts.

I've been an observer of leaders in community organizations and the business sector for years. I've tried to learn what works from the best of them and incorporate it into my organizations. And I've tried to avoid what doesn't work. Those lessons accumulated over the years, and I found they emerged in conversation with Franca. We both hope they are helpful to others interested in leadership and successful organizations.

FRANCA GUCCIARDI: The first person I want to thank is my co-author and mentor, Alan, for his supportive ear and insightful questions throughout my tenure as a CEO as well as for his patience in letting me set the (slow) place of writing this book while I juggled being both a new CEO and a new mom. Thank you to Vali Bennett for keeping us on course (not to mention her friendship throughout these years).

The first CEO I observed in my life was Bob Cluett. Without him there would be no Loran Scholars Foundation. His clarity on the mission and his determination to realize it were perhaps the most important lesson. Additionally, without him, I fear I might have ended up as a tax lawyer (not that there is anything wrong with that!). He believed in my potential when I was still in my teens and gave me every opportunity to realize it. I am forever in his debt. Over the course of my tenure at Loran, I had the chance to learn from many people, particularly the outstanding board directors and the seven chairs of the board with whom I worked. Their commitment to Loran's growth and development have helped support much of the work described in this book.

Many kind people read versions of this book at different stages and provided their constructive feedback including Tina Edan, Jesse Helmer, Julia Lo, and Lindsey Li. Markus Stadelmann-Elder was nothing short of a superstar in finally getting this project completed. Thank you to my friends and family for their support. A special thank you to my husband, Alex Usher, for telling me the truth on how to improve the early drafts (especially when I didn't want to hear it) and for encouraging me to write this book in the first place. And especially to my Giulia, thank you for your unending joy.

ABOUT THE AUTHORS

ALAN BROADBENT

Alan Broadbent is Chairman and CEO of Avana Capital Corporation and chairman of Maytree, a charity committed to advancing systemic solutions to poverty and strengthening civic communities.

He has co-founded and chairs a number of initiatives including the Caledon Institute of Social Policy, Tamarack – An Institute for Community Engagement, and the Institute on Municipal Finance and Governance at the Munk School of Global Affairs, University of Toronto. In addition, he is a Director of Sustainalytics Holdings B.V., Chair of the Toronto Inner-City Rugby Foundation, Senior Fellow and Chair of the Governing Board of Massey College, Member of the

Governors' Council of the Toronto Public Library Foundation, and board member at JAZZ.FM.

Alan is the author of *Urban Nation: Why We Need to Give Power Back to the Cities to Make Canada Strong*, and co-editor of *Five Good Ideas: Practical Strategies for Non-Profit Success*, and was awarded an honorary Doctor of Laws degree from Ryerson University in 2009, and from Queen's University in 2015.

He is a Member of the Order of Canada and recipient of the Queen's Diamond Jubilee Medal.

FRANCA GUCCIARDI

Since 2004, Franca Gucciardi has served as CEO of the Loran Scholars Foundation, a charity that identifies exceptional young Canadians who demonstrate character, service, and leadership and funds them to study at Canadian universities. To date, 569 past and present Loran Scholars have benefited from the foundation's world-class enrichment programs.

Franca grew up in Sicily and immigrated with her family to Toronto in the 1980s. She obtained a BA from the University of Waterloo as one of the first Loran Scholars to be selected in 1990. She also holds an MA from Carleton University's Norman Paterson School of International Affairs as well as the Chartered Director designation from The Directors College.

After five years as the Founding Director of Canada's Millennium Excellence Awards, Franca rejoined the Loran family as CEO in 2004. In her first year, she led the organization to double its assets from just over half a million dollars to $1.4 million. Twelve years later, Loran is the top undergraduate scholarship program in the country with assets of $13 million. In the intervening time, Franca stewarded the foundation through several development phases, and it continues to grow and offer a greater number of awards and opportunities to scholars and alumni than ever before. Franca will join the McCall MacBain Foundation as its CEO in the fall of 2017.

In the community, Franca holds roles as board chair of College Montrose Children's Place and board director with the McGill Institute for the Study of Canada. She is also a member of the Leadership Council of the Ian O. Ihnatowycz Institute for Leadership. She previously served as vice-chair of the board of directors of Volunteer Canada and as chair of its public policy committee.

Franca was one of thirty-three women named a Fellow of the International Women's Forum in 2013. She is the 2015 recipient of the Gil Bennett Gold Standard Governance Award and the Sara Kirke Award for Entrepreneurship and Innovation.

What is culture of Metcalf?

What does it value most?

what are staff good at, what motivates them, outcomes

<u>Q:</u> Strengths + short comings of organization

⊗ Access to personnel files
× Staff Meetings (118)
(P.101) - questions from staff upon beginning.

   ★ Create Org. Chart of Organization

×× × Firing (p. $\begin{smallmatrix}106\\107\\108\end{smallmatrix}$)

   × Staff Code of Conduct (111)

- Underperforming (111)
- Performance Reviews (114)

- Staff retreat (116)